D0629651

a beautiful defeat

a beautiful defeat

Find True Freedom and Purpose
in Total Surrender to God

Kevin Malarkey

with Matt Jacobson

NELSON
BOOKS

An Imprint of Thomas Nelson

Published in Nashville, Tennessee, by Nelson Books, an imprint of Thomas Nelson. Nelson Books and Thomas Nelson are registered trademarks of HarperCollins Christian Publishing, Inc.

Published in association with the Loyal Arts Literary Agency.

Thomas Nelson titles may be purchased in bulk for educational, business, fund-raising, or sales promotional use. For information, please e-mail SpecialMarkets@ThomasNelson.com.

Unless otherwise noted, Scripture quotations are taken from the Holy Bible, New International Version®, NIV®. Copyright © 1973, 1978, 1984, 2011 by Biblica, Inc.™ Used by permission of Zondervan. All rights reserved worldwide. www.zondervan.com.

Scripture quotations marked NKJV are taken from the NEW KING JAMES VERSION. © 1982 by Thomas Nelson, Inc. Used by permission. All rights reserved.

Scripture quotations marked NASB are taken from the NEW AMERICAN STANDARD BIBLE®, © The Lockman Foundation 1960, 1962, 1963, 1968, 1971, 1972, 1973, 1975, 1977, 1995. Used by permission.

Scripture quotations marked MSG are taken from The Message by Eugene H. Peterson. © 1993, 1994, 1995, 1996, 2000. Used by permission of NavPress Publishing Group. All rights reserved.

Scripture quotations marked NLT are taken from the Holy Bible, New Living Translation. © 1996. Used by permission of Tyndale House Publishers, Inc., Wheaton, Illinois 60189. All rights reserved.

Scripture quotations marked KJV are taken from the King James Version. Public domain.

**The Library of Congress Cataloging-in-Publication Data
is on file with the Library of Congress.**

ISBN: 978-1-4002-0639-1

Printed in the United States of America

14 15 16 17 18 RRD 6 5 4 3 2 1

To the DeLong Family:
Danton, Melia, Aramis, Jubilee, Hosannah, and Nalani

*Direct me in the path of your commands,
for there I find delight.*

—PSALM 119:35

Contents

Introduction

This Is Going to Get Messy

I'D RATHER HAVE A ROOT CANAL WITHOUT anesthetic than get real and reveal my struggles. Not the ones we're happy to mention for prayer on Sunday morning, but the other ones—the ones that good Christians aren't supposed to have, the ones that ensure you won't be invited to the Saturday barbecue or that make people keep it light and short when talking with you.

There's a powerful force in me that wants to do anything but get real and reveal the part of me that's been diminished by sin. I feel it when I am alone and don't want others to know what I'm thinking or feeling. I feel it when I'm talking to friends and purposefully withhold a key piece of information because I know and fear they will think less of me.

It's a lesson you learn quickly from the average Christian gathering: everyone thinks you're more spiritual if there is no hint of struggle or failure in your life—or if the struggles are of an "acceptable" nature. So we learn to just keep smiling and not "go there."

But there's a deeper, more authentic voice calling to me than the one that says to hide, evade, or redirect the conversation to safe territory. What you are about to read starts in a different place—the truth about my life . . . and about yours. I'm going to reveal some things about myself that may change the way you look at me . . . and not in a good way. In fact, humanly speaking, it probably makes more sense to just be quiet about *all that*. Who wants their failures, shortcomings, and, well, sin, to be paraded around? But I'm willing to risk it. Though it's messy, I'm going to stake everything on the belief that our path to God is through and with our struggles, not by sidestepping or hiding them.

I would also like to speak against an unspoken belief that is found in both our culture and in the church: that struggle in life and in following Christ is always a sign of having done something wrong. I like to say it this way: he who has the least struggles is not the better person. In fact, in many places the Bible makes a case for quite the opposite. Jesus himself led a perfect life, but his ministry was filled with conflict and struggle. The goal should be obedience and surrender to God rather than a path that has no obstacles.

We say that we want to live for God. We want to give our lives over to him. And then we spend most of our time trying to put him out of business. Is it not considered a good day if you are able to buy into the illusion that you did not need him?

I'm not coming into this discussion as someone who has this "surrender" thing down to a science or a simple, neat math equation. I'm on a pilgrimage that involves a real life lived in the real world, full of real mistakes and a merciful God who doesn't give me a pass on sin but does give me grace to take the next step. I have, however, found some principles that have been helpful for me. At the end of each chapter, I will summarize the chapter into one of ten concepts that I have found help me to try to lead a surrendered life. I will also provide you with an action step and a sample prayer to aid you in your quest to surrender more and more of your life to God.

The first step comes from this introduction:

FIRST STEP TO A SURRENDERED LIFE: Know that the process of surrender is messy.

Action Step

Determine not to control your process of surrender. Commit to be open to whatever God and those close to you begin to show you. Do not try to align everything in the beginning of the process, but let things come together naturally for you further down the line.

Prayer

Father, help me not to chain myself to a vision of perfection. Teach me that I do not have to clean myself up to approach you. You know everything about me, so help me give all of it to you that you may make it clean. There is no reason for me to hold on to all that is tormenting me. Help me understand that struggle is a part of life that is not always an indicator of my disobedience. When I do act in ways that I should not, please forgive me. And when my hard times have nothing to do with my actions, please keep my mind and heart free to hear from you.

Has your life gotten confusing and your struggles intense? Maybe you view your life as one big disappointment and not what you first thought when you came to faith. I'm hoping you'll find me honest—and in so doing, you'll be able to be honest too. And you will be able to admit that you're not in control even though you still live and make choices as if you were calling the shots. We try so hard to win the battle for control that our efforts actually lead to increased frustration. This is the crux of something vital that prevents us from finding true peace and wholeness. Let me share a life with you that is better than much of what is found in the twenty-first-century church, a perspective that makes sense of the mess and is filled with richness and purpose for today . . . and hope for tomorrow.

Part I

A CALL FOR AUTHENTICITY

One

Our Dirty Little Secrets

NOW, ABOUT THAT CONFESSION—THE FACT IS, I'm not a good person.

Please don't think, *Oh, he's just saying that.* Left to myself, I'm capable of just about anything, and when I fail, believe me, it's memorable. I'm embarrassed to say it, but I was a drunk for two years in college. Oh, I maintained high grades and respectability most of the time, but the fact is, I was frequently drunk. I'm often fearful that I won't ever be the man I want my sons to become or the type of guy I would want my daughter to marry. I often lack self-confidence, and I try way too hard to get people to like me. Sometimes I even wonder if I am capable of reflecting the God whom I say inhabits my heart.

———

"Hey, what do you say to checking out where I went to college?"

"Definitely, Dad, let's do it!"

Mile after mile passed by while the radio remained silent, but it was music to my ears and heart. We just talked. I love that about our relationship. My son is twelve and still loves to talk to me. I'm a blessed dad! We talked a bit about faith and a bit about his various interests. We then talked about how faith and our lives are to be intertwined and not separate from each other. Conversations like this one don't happen all the time between my son and me, but on this morning, I began to feel like quite the godly father.

We arrived at my college campus, and it was a beautiful day to walk around and see the sights. I showed him the places I lived, where I attended classes, the student center, everything. You'd have thought we were in DC looking at the monuments. He was completely enthralled.

"I want to go to college here, Dad!"

Now, I loved my school, but there was a part of me that always hoped he'd go somewhere else. Was that because I wanted him to chart his own course? Maybe. But mainly, it was because the memories of my first couple of years in college were as fresh as yesterday. I did not want this to happen to him. Okay, it didn't "happen" to me—I made choices, bad ones, and somehow this place made it seem that it could happen to him too. Not very logical, but there it is.

And then it happened.

He pointed at a building.

"Hey, Dad, did you ever do anything in that building?"

It was the campus chapel.

"Oh, definitely!" I said, deflecting the fear that instantly gripped my chest. "I heard Jesse Jackson speak in there, went to a few concerts and some other things."

But my mind was racing. In it? . . . Yeah, I did some things in it. On it . . . that was the real issue suddenly confronting this "godly" father's conscience.

I hesitated. As parents, we don't want our children to lose respect for us or think less of us. Should I risk it? Should I tell my twelve-year-old my most vivid memory of that building? Do I want to untie the knot on the bow of that package? What would he think of me then? If you're listening to the Holy Spirit, you're not writing the script, but you are called to follow. I decided to tell my son the truth.

"Son," I said, taking in a deep breath, "I actually climbed up on top of that roof and hung a sign for the fraternity that I was in. I'm not going to tell you what was on that sign, but it wasn't good. You see that pathway where you could climb up? That's where I got up. After I hung the sign I dumped water down on that area so that it would freeze and no one could get up there to take the sign down."

"Why did you do that? What's a fraternity?"

Open a door and it's going to lead somewhere. I continued to open up with my son and honestly answered his questions, sharing about fraternities, mine in particular—famous for binge drinking and not much studying. He didn't seem surprised when I confessed I wound up on academic and social probation. In less than a year, I had two DUIs to my credit.

"Son, I was so lost at that point in my life, striving to find something I didn't even understand I was looking for. Fact is, I had abandoned my faith even though if you asked me at the time, I would say to anyone, 'Oh yeah, I'm a Christian.'" I also told him the weird thing was that I actually considered this a great time while I was doing it. I had a ton of "friends" and remember feeling quite happy. (Anyone who tells you sin isn't fun or pleasurable, in the moment, is lying. Even the Bible speaks of the pleasure of sin for a season.)

There, I did it. I stopped my story and turned to my son, bracing for his response. You've got to understand, he really looks up to me. Had I said too much? Fear crept in . . . Had I compromised all this?

"Wow, Dad!" He grinned. "God is awesome!"

"What? What do you mean?" I asked, surprised, stunned even, though trying not to show it.

"Look at you now. He is so amazing!"

Now that's some seriously wild stuff from a twelve-year-old. Instead of seeing "Dad the failure," he saw God the redeemer! His focus was on how far God had brought me, not on how far I had fallen. Being honest with my son about my scarred past had no impact on his view of me but deepened his faith in what God can do. Had I listened to the voice of fear, I might have missed it all.

My son's response also reminded me of how an improper perspective on struggle can get in the way of what God would most likely desire to get from our difficult times—mainly, glory for himself. Our incessant need to look good (even when we are not so good) hides our deep need for him and in turn does not allow others to see the great things he has done for us.

We are all better off being honest about our struggles, choosing to depend on God, and then giving him credit for the improvement that follows.

I'm glad I risked it that day instead of letting fear keep me from the deeper relationship with my son God had planned for that day. This is the power of authenticity in relationship. Will we risk our pride for God's glory?

Is God asking you to take a risk?

But maybe you think my story is safe because it is in the past. How about this:

I am the at-fault driver in an accident that caused one of my children to be paralyzed.

Want more?

I've struggled with pornography. My house has been in foreclosure. I have made some sizable contributions to broken relationships. There have been many painful moments when the decisions I made poorly and quickly have led to a lifetime of consequences. And these things all happened *after* I made a genuine decision to follow Christ.

God wants to meet us now, in the challenges, struggles, failures, and shortcomings of today.

Like Karen.

It was a speaking event following the publication of my first book. I was not practiced in these things and wasn't sure what to expect. The winter weather didn't keep people away from Northway Church in Pittsburgh that Saturday evening, though. In minutes, the auditorium filled with well over one thousand people. I felt like keeping my interview with the pastor on safe territory, listening to the "reasonable" voice that says "hide" and "evade."

But then I felt a deeper, more authentic voice. I made a decision: Tonight there will be no prepackaged presentation of self. It will just be real. If God brings a personal weakness to mind (he did), I will share it. If a story gets messy and off track (it happened), I will not try to make sense of it. The interview that night was without notes and focused purely on connecting with God and the audience at our deepest point of need. It was uncomfortable at first. And then something amazing happened.

After the interview, a line of over one hundred people formed in the lobby to talk with me and have me sign their books. As I began meeting people, the turn of the conversation surprised me. Over and over again, people would share their struggles and their pain with me. They all began by saying something like, "I have never told anyone this before, but . . ." People opened up, letting down the barricade between their hearts and me.

After quite a long time, the line wasn't getting any shorter and I became conscious of the need to keep things moving.

And then she caught my eye.

About three people behind the person I was speaking with, a woman stood, crying openly. It was difficult to keep my eyes focused on the person in front of me. The woman crying seemed the type that typically had things under control—she was dressed in a way that projected confidence. When she finally got to the front of the line, she was still crying but was attempting to regain her composure.

understand about the hardest things you face, the struggles that cut you down, humiliate, debilitate, and impede your progress while piercing your heart with pain and sorrow. You can make it because he is there. He knows, he understands, and he will never give up on you. But to experience what he has to offer, you have to not only come to him but come to him his way.

And his way is to make a clean confession of your messes and to relax your hands, giving up the control that you don't really have but deceive yourself into believing you do.

Through my years of being a counselor, I think it's safe to say I've heard just about every dirty secret there is. But as I sat there year after year, a reality, a fact, came clearer and clearer into focus: I was no different from the people I was helping. I had dirty laundry too. And as I revealed above, it's not all in the past tense. I still struggle, I still mess up, I still make mistakes—just like everyone, from the superpastor of the megachurch to the janitor who cleans the restrooms, to the faithful housewife, to the missionary in West Africa—to everyone.

If you're like me, like most people, you have faced or are facing some challenging times. Maybe you're hurt, stressed, or under immense pressure. Are you bitterly ashamed of what you've done or in some other deeply emotional turmoil? Maybe it's of your own making, maybe not, but you are struggling and in the tougher moments, it feels like you are flying solo—alone in this world.

Before you take one step further, I want you to ask yourself a question: Why did I pick up this book?

I think I may know the answer.

You are not satisfied with where your Christian life has

taken you. You know you are missing something—something that, intuitively, you know you were intended to have.

And you want it badly. You want something more, something deep and something that says to you that there is purpose and meaning. Even though you've prayed the "sinner's prayer," you haven't yet found all you were looking for, but you want to.

The starting point in this journey is honesty—honesty with God. Do you still like to pretend he does not know everything about you? Someone once said that to be a good writer all you have to do is to open a vein and bleed. I think that's what it takes (metaphorically) to be a good pray-er. Will you get honest with God? Will you open your heart and bleed?

Our loving Father wants us to come to him with every pain, burden, challenge, and mess. Will you bare your soul before God, confess where you really are at with life—your struggles, temptations, messes, and difficulties—and invite God to take his rightful place in your life?

———

Before we're ready to move ahead, we need to reevaluate a few things.

Even if you've never thought about it before, you have a pretty specific idea about how the Christian life should work. Most of us need to change our minds about that. We often begin our faith pilgrimage thinking it's a smooth walk to the Celestial City now that we are on the correct path. Haven't we all been told for years that God has a wonderful plan for our lives? After all, aren't hard times for people who are doing life wrong—for those who stray off the beaten path? Aren't difficult relationships for people who are fatally flawed?

It doesn't help when believers imply that the Christian life is always an easier road compared to that of the nonbeliever, or that once you are a true Christ-follower, you are on the road to perfection. One look at the Bible destroys this myth. Do I need to remind you about Peter (the Rock?) who turned his back on Jesus *after* following him for several years (Matt. 26:69–75)—or how he opposed God's way *after* the resurrection (Acts 10:9–16)? I could tell you story after story of disciples, apostles, and believers who struggled . . . and struggled again . . . to live the life of faith. We have something important to learn from this reality: facing struggle isn't a one-shot deal.

For you, for me, for every Christian, struggle is here to stay. Just when I've gotten through a crisis, ready for a little R & R from the challenge, I'm faced with another struggle. The question isn't, Will it happen? but, When it happens, will I come clean with God and, again, relinquish my control, inviting him into every corner of my life?

Remember, you are not alone. Even though your struggles can take you to a lonely place, you are not the only person who struggles. Whether it's the picture-perfect family in the front pew at church, the put-together single business woman who seemingly has need of nothing and no one, or the perfect pastor whom no one will open up to because of the aura of perfection he carefully projects, or me . . . it doesn't matter. Everyone is facing something that is uniquely personal to him and universal to everyone else. So, change your mind on what you are expecting of the Christian life. You're going to "do" struggle. The question is, will you struggle well?

And there's something else we need to change. We need to change our minds about the kind of God we worship. If we were to look inside people's minds, including most Christians, and learn their ideas about God, we'd find basically the same thing. The picture isn't pretty. We'd find a big, grumpy guy with a lot of power, sourly reviewing the lives of believers as he finds endless reasons to disapprove. Though not a biblical image, let's face it. Most people live with the nagging suspicion that God is constantly angry or disappointed with them.

Somehow we've come to believe that difficult life circumstances are for people who have made God angry. What else can we conclude? Makes sense, doesn't it? The hard times we are facing are a disapproving God's special path of punishment for us.

In the midst of the fog of confusion obscuring everything but the immediate crisis we are dealing with, where is the God who is willing to help me get rid of all this trauma if . . .

He really loved me?

Have you ever asked yourself, "If God really loved me, would this be happening?" I know I have. And most of us can hear the answer reverberating in our heads: "Of course not. God doesn't love you, not right now—not in this state of failure, of shortcoming, of impossible physical or financial hardship. When God loves people . . . when God loves you . . . things like this don't happen. When God approves of you, he gives you favor to excel, to achieve, and to avoid the problems of sinners.

Well, if this is true, then I have another confession to make: I'm a sinner

- who God doesn't love,
- with whom God is angry, and
- of whom God doesn't approve.

Thank goodness this is not how things really are.

It's time for you to change your mind about God.

The Bible says God is there, all the time—that he won't leave you or forsake you. So why does it feel like you've been forsaken and forgotten by an almighty God? Where was he in that last storm you just weathered, or why can't you see him in the one on the horizon? If we want the truth, we have to not only get our information from the right source but embrace that truth when we find it.

Maybe you just don't have the will to believe there is a possibility of raising your head above the drowning waves. You've been burnt too many times. You've disappointed too many people. You've failed so often, you don't think you will ever find victory. Have you given up on yourself? That's okay. There were many times in the Bible when people gave up, despairing that God would help them. Are you feeling something similar?

Still, it's okay.

Why?

Because God hasn't given up on you! And we need to remember, as great as the view is from the barren rocks at the top of the mountain, all the lush growth is down in the valley of life.

Even in the midst of the deepest distress, of the deepest struggle, God's purposes are at work. We are all going to struggle, even if we aren't in the midst of a storm right now. God wants us to learn to struggle well. Will you let him show you how?

It's a journey we can take together because, brother, sister, I'm not talking down from some ivory tower. I'm on the trail with you hacking my way through tangled growth.

And while on this journey, regardless of the nature of our struggles and failures, we need to learn an important truth: God is less interested in where we fell than he is in what we choose to do next.

SECOND STEP TO A SURRENDERED LIFE: Be honest about your existing struggles.

Action Step

Make a list of the things in your life and about yourself that you really do not like. Write down what it is costing you to leave each issue unresolved. Begin to think about what it would be like to have peace in these areas even if the circumstances never change.

Prayer

Father, please help me more deeply understand that I do not need to perform for you. It is hard for me to believe that you designed me exactly the way you wanted me made. I worry more about what other people think they know about me than what you say is true about me. I want to let go of every burden, but I often find myself holding on tighter when I get scared.

Lord, where do you want me to start?

Show me one thing in my life that I can start with, and give me the courage to let go and turn it over to you. Help me learn to trust that being real with you and yielding my heart to you is always in my best interest. Thank you for loving and accepting me as I am.

So, where do our struggles really come from?

Two

Where Our Struggles Really Come From (Part 1)

Recently, I took my ten-year-old daughter to her softball game, the end-of-the-year tournament. It promised to be an exciting day (she's an amazing pitcher!) but also a long, hot, and humid one. You see, whether she won or lost her morning game of this double-elimination tournament, her team would be playing more games in the afternoon. And there was a good chance that she could play three or even four games. My daughter's team was pretty good, and, of course, my little girl is the best softball player on earth!

Everyone knows Little League sports have a way of turning normally reasonable parents into complete morons. It never occurred to me that today might be my turn. We lost the first game, but I was feeling good because a "God moment" happened and I got into a conversation with a fellow believer about the role of worship music in our lives. Don't you just love it when God does that?

As the day moved into the early afternoon hours, we won the second game, which meant we would begin game number three twenty-five minutes later . . . in the high humidity and eighty-five-degree heat. My daughter pitched every inning of the first two games and was scheduled to pitch as much as she could in the third game. I spent most of the first six hours of the tournament being a good dad, making sure she was well hydrated and preserving her energy by staying in the shade as much as possible.

The third game began badly. An extremely controversial call based on a rule none of our coaches had ever heard of resulted in one of our base runners being called out. I don't mind losing a call or even a game if things are fair, but it makes me crazy when random calls like this are made. You might say I began watching the game with even more intensity (as if that were possible!).

During the next inning my daughter inadvertently dropped the softball just as she was beginning to pitch.

"*Ball!*" the ump called out in a purposefully irritating "gotcha" voice (not really, but that's how it sounded at the time, with the ears I had on). Now, for the record, this was the correct call, but I wanted justice and yelled loud enough for everyone to hear, "You didn't call 'ball' when their player did that." You could see the umpire's body instantly freeze. He turned slowly and gave me a deadpan look with a voice to match. "I was not in position in that situation." I didn't say anything, but looked away and thought to myself, *Yeah, and whose fault was that, big guy?*

Folding my arms and breathing deeply, I settled down a

bit as our team soon took a comfortable lead. My daughter was spectacular, pitching a shutout through three innings! I began to smile with the "that's my daughter out there" look.

Excellent, we won! Both teams lined up to shake hands at the end of the third inning because the coaches had felt the time constraints of the tournament meant there was not time to play another entire inning. This would be a good thing for all concerned as the heat and humidity of the afternoon bore down on everyone. The players were especially glad the game was finally over . . . or so everyone thought. The umpire glanced at his watch and then yelled, "Everyone, back on the field."

Apparently there were five minutes to allow the start of another inning. We were well ahead and there was no way the other team could accomplish anything in one inning that would change the result. Having to endure the heat and humidity was miserable, but the umpire was in charge, so the players returned to the field and the parents continued to bake a little longer in the sun.

Our girls scored six more runs in the top of the inning and now had a double-digit lead and needed only three outs in the bottom of the inning to secure the victory. Early in the inning, my daughter threw a pitch I thought was a strike.

"*Ball!*" the umpire called. (Was he yelling it in my face?)

Everyone knows that you can't accurately assess a pitch unless you're standing in the position of the umpire, directly behind the catcher, but that little fact didn't keep me from becoming one of "those" parents. I shouted out to no one in particular, "Really?"

The umpire froze, then slowly turned, looking at me. "Are you talking to me?"

Surprised to suddenly be in a one-on-one conversation that everyone in the stands was listening to, I replied, "Yes."

He pointed his index finger directly at me and said, "One more word from you and you are out of here."

My anger began to seethe but I didn't say anything . . . until the game ended a few minutes later. As the girls were going to shake hands again, I saw from the corner of my eye the umpire coming through our dugout on the way to his car. I shouldn't have said anything, but I couldn't resist. I walked straight toward him and asked, "What's the problem with saying 'really' regarding one of your calls?"

"Well, maybe I can explain it to you. The problem is, it was an obvious ball—right at the knees but outside, which you couldn't possibly have judged accurately from where you were sitting."

But my anger wasn't really about the pitch. It was about my pride. I didn't like being called out during the game, and I hate being talked down to . . . the way he was talking to me right now.

"Look," I said, staring directly into his eyes, "you are outside of the fence now. You don't need to talk to me that way." (At least this is what I think I said.)

"Are you threatening me?" he angrily called out for everyone to hear. "Hey, everyone, this guy is threatening me!"

Immediately sensing the situation was about to escalate and get out of hand, several dads moved casually between us. Just then, one of the assistant coaches started yelling.

"What is your problem? It's parents like you who set a bad example for everyone. It's just a game."

Another dad weighed in with disgust. "Hey, c'mon guys, the girls are still on the field shaking hands."

And now it was all too late. Parents started uncomfortably looking for their keys and filtering away. Emotionally, the scene was like the aftermath of a tornado—random destruction everywhere you looked and a sick feeling settling somewhere deep in your gut. Embarrassment engulfed me. Who was the problem parent making a scene—the one we all want to avoid?

Uh . . . that would be me. I was that guy . . . the guy the parents would talk about on their rides home wondering, "What is wrong with him?"

Did I embarrass my daughter?

Did I have to ask?

What, exactly, just happened?

My initial inward reactions were typical male: *What is that umpire's problem? I can't believe that coach yelled at me. I used to go to church with him. What a jerk.* During the next couple of hours, the scene played over and over in my mind. How did this situation occur? I never meant to insult anyone. I didn't use any bad language. I was not upset about the outcome of the game. The only thing I was really mad about was how that ump talked to me and that this assistant coach yelled at me.

So how did I become the jerk? In a word: *sin.*

The word *sin* is a lot like the word *cancer*—it describes a lot of different things, all of them bad. All of them destructive.

But we have to understand this three-letter powerhouse better than we do. Because understanding where the attacks are coming from is one of the critical keys to walking closer to God.

The Bible says that there are three sources of our sin: the flesh, the world, and the devil. In other words: you, where you live, and who runs the place. Of course, my "flesh" had a lot to do with my being such an idiot at the softball game—and I am going to get to that (even though I don't want to!). But I want to start with the devil because he is such a neglected aspect in the teaching of many churches today.

Outside of horror film lovers (of which I'm not), our culture considers, for the most part, Satan and the idea of some malevolent force in the spiritual realm as a complete joke— the leftover superstition of an uneducated, base existence now thankfully lost in the mists of time. No educated person takes seriously the idea of Satan as a real, living, destructive person. That's the stuff of fantasy and ignorance.

The Bible has a different take than the culture—a real shocker, I know. But how many of us really think through the implications of what the Bible says about the archenemy of mankind? Do we even know what it says? If we do, we'd better take it seriously. If we don't, we'd better find out.

The Bible gives Satan a lot of names, all painting a grim picture of the enemy of our souls. The reason these names have particular significance for the Christian is because the implications of the names have no bearing on God. He's above it all, but we are not. Satan will be who he is—not a big concern if you happen to be Jehovah, but more to the point, Satan will be who he is to you and me. This is why his names have particular bearing on what we understand and how we walk.

What are those names? Here's a short list: accuser (of you and me), destroyer, adversary, deceiver, father of lies, murderer, roaring lion, ruler of demons, ruler of this world, thief, tempter, serpent of old.

There are many other names for the enemy of our souls, but seriously, how many do we need? It's not a pretty picture. The question is, will we believe it? Do you take Satan seriously? It's easy to think of him as the enemy of our souls in the abstract, but do you really see him as an active, destructive force for evil in your daily life? From the beginning, when Eve fell to temptation in the garden and Adam went along with her, Satan's opposition to everything God is and does is well cataloged in the Bible—and Satan plays for keeps. He's a deceiver and a killer.

As a deceiver, he'll try to convince you that that relational struggle you're having is just about you and the person giving you fits; as an accuser, he'll tell you that you're guilty of the sin God has already forgiven; as a liar, he will claim that God is displeased with you and doesn't love you; as a thief, he'll rob you of joy; as a roaring lion, he'll try to paralyze your spirit with fear so he can feast on your flesh; as the tempter, he'll throw in your path whatever it takes to bring you shame, defeat, desolation; as the destroyer, he will destroy everything that's good, everything that's fruitful, everything that speaks of God.

"For we wrestle not against flesh and blood, but against principalities, against powers, against the rulers of the darkness of this world, against spiritual wickedness in high places" (Eph. 6:12 KJV).

Do we take this reality seriously?

The other day I was watching a TV preacher parade across the stage taunting Satan like some cat with a wounded bird, encouraging the crowd to mock him because, as the guy explained, Satan is a proud spirit who can't stand being mocked. It wasn't the first time I had seen a display like this, but it still made me cringe. Is that all Satan really is—some helpless wounded bird we can slap around?

If he's such a pathetic adversary for someone walking the Christian life, why are we told to be alert and sober because he is prowling around like a roaring lion, looking for someone to eat (1 Peter 5:8)? Why does the Bible refer to "the wiles [cunning deceitfulness] of the devil" (Eph. 6:11 NKJV)? Why are we told to be on guard against his deception and temptations?

The TV preacher wanted everyone to think of Satan as some toothless old lion. Try telling that to the early Christians ripped limb from limb by real lions in the Roman coliseum, the result of Satan's efforts. Satan as decrepit and powerless is fiction. He's still destroying, still deceiving, still devouring. Satan is still a formidable adversary. Satan's activity in this world and in your life is deadly serious. We don't have to fear him, but he's not to be trifled with.

When attacked by the evil one, the apostle James tells believers to resist the devil and he will flee from them (James 4:7). Nowhere in the Bible are believers instructed to take the devil head-on, not even Michael the archangel—the leader of the armies of heaven. What does this most powerful warrior angel do? Jude 1:9 explains, "But even the archangel Michael, when he was disputing with the devil about the body of Moses, did not himself dare to condemn him for slander but said, 'The Lord rebuke you!'"

When it comes to Satan, let's allow the Lord to do the direct fighting. We are told to resist. Jesus allowed the Lord to fight for him as well. Remember when Satan came to tempt Jesus in his hour of extreme physical weakness after his long fast? What did he do? Certainly not all he could have! Even though he had the power to summon more than twelve legions of angels (Matt. 26:53), when contending with the devil, Jesus merely spoke the words of his Father, the words of Scripture, as his answer. He resisted. It was enough. Satan fled, as we are promised he will do when we resist him.

Now, you have to admit, it makes for better TV to have some guy in a nine-hundred-dollar suit, diamond-studded cufflinks, and alligator shoes strutting across the stage, showing the wildly cheering crowd how spiritually tough he is by yelling insults at Satan, but when it comes to dealing with Satan in our everyday lives, we'd do better to follow Jesus' and Michael's examples rather than some faith healer who can't heal his own hair.

Enemy #1 in this spiritual war we see unfolding through the struggles of our lives is Satan himself. We don't need to walk in fear of him, but we need to be on our guard, taking seriously his deadly serious purposes and activity in our lives.

I hurt.

I hurt because I have made a lot of bad mistakes, the consequences of which dog me to this very day. I hurt because of too many bad relationships along with more hard circumstances than I ever imagined for my life. But mostly, I hurt because that's what this place called Earth does to you. It inflicts pain—that's what enemies do. They hurt you if they can. That's why the Bible says Enemy #2 is the world. Where we live is our enemy.

We can paint on a smile and keep going, but no matter how you dress it up, sweet babies die of leukemia, bitter divorces break up beautiful families, out-of-control governments kill and maim, destructive natural disasters take the lives of thousands, and random violence erupts constantly in the most peaceful neighborhoods.

If you are not hurting emotionally and/or physically right now, you have in your past and you certainly will again. If you're young and life is looking to you like one extended party . . . give it a little more time. Life is hard and the good times are fleeting. Even when the fog of pain begins to lift, the truth is, we really don't have the answers to most of the problems life presents, but we can be confident they will continue to come.

There have been times (and maybe you've been there too) that emptiness and purposelessness roll over me like a wave far above my head, first engulfing me, then picking me up and slamming my body down on the hard-packed sand. Tension comes; short, anxious breaths persist; and for a moment, the logic of swimming out to sea makes perfect sense to me.

No matter how much this world gives us, the older and wiser we get, we start to suspect that it's all an effort to hide from us the real issue—that the world has nothing of true substance to offer. What, exactly, is it that we don't have but desperately desire? On the one hand, there's a gnawing inside that tells us we just might find it if we could have a little bit more, if we could just get a break, be recognized, get healthier, work a little harder, make a little more money, or break free from that one sin or struggle—then everything in life would improve.

But, eventually, and usually after toying with us a bit, life forces us to realize that rainbows are an illusion and we come face-to-face with a hard truth: there's no rainbow, and there's no gold because illusions can't provide the real thing.

The world does not satisfy—not that we don't listen to the lie and strive after its empty promises. It has its moments, some of which surpass incredible. But taken as a whole, if we are honest, the whole thing is a major-league letdown. The world does not have the capacity to satisfy our most basic inner craving—a longing that is so natural to how we think and feel but somehow remains out of reach.

Maybe it sounds like I've been describing "nonbelievers"—people who don't know Jesus—but I'm not. I'm talking about the vast majority of those who call themselves Christians. Non-Christians do not have a monopoly on emptiness, purpose-lessness, and a life devoid of peace. We Christians too often find ourselves struggling with these things and that growing feeling that we're missing something we shouldn't. It's like we're living inside U2's song "I Still Haven't Found What I'm Looking For." For someone who has said yes to Jesus' offer of mercy and grace, it almost seems blasphemous to allow yourself to think this way, but seriously, how many Christians do you know who don't, from time to time, struggle with these feelings?

Don't get me wrong, I understand perfectly that Christian religious culture dictates we're not supposed to let on that there's anything wrong. When it comes to life's struggles—a spiritual life that resembles the Gobi desert, or fear about an uncertain future—we may be dying on the inside, but we'll keep smiling at our friends, quoting Scripture to each other, and singing all the latest worship tunes. We know we aren't living a life that even comes close to resembling the descriptions we find in the Bible.

> May the God of hope fill you with all joy and peace as you trust in him, so that you may overflow with hope by the power of the Holy Spirit. (Rom. 15:13)

> I have come that they may have life, and that they may have it more abundantly. (John 10:10 NKJV)

So, what's the disconnect? I don't want to live like that. Actually, does anyone? Who doesn't want to find the path of peace, joy, and abundant life through this journey we call life? The Bible says it's a narrow way and only a few find it. I want to be one of those few. I want to find it. I don't want the counterfeit offered up by twenty-first-century religion that has all the words right along with some great music but doesn't provide what the Bible promises. It's either true or it isn't. I don't want a Christian life that looks great on paper but produces anxiety, emptiness, and despair amidst an ocean of smiles and shallow relationships an inch deep.

What is the secret to having your back lacerated in a beating, being placed in shackles, and then spending the night so filled with peace and joy, confident in what God was doing (or not doing), that you just couldn't keep from singing songs of praise like Paul and Silas? That's the faith I want. Something so authentic, so real, it keeps me in a place of praise in the midst of life's best efforts at taking me down. How about you?

Wouldn't it be great if it was possible?

It's confusing. Bad stuff happens—bad stuff that is completely out of our control and not of our making. This is all the result of a world in the grip and under the power of sin, and the Bible describes anyone who loves it as God's enemy (James 4:4).

Our God cares about what we love.

Taken together, this is the world under sin and Satan—all thinking and action that is antithetical to God's law, God's love, and God's purposes in the world—bringing struggle, pain, and hardship to every true believer and to everyone else.

But we're not going in blind. The Bible is clear and specific when it comes to the perspective on the world we are expected to have as we live within the system: Don't love it. Don't love the things that are in it.

First John 2:15 says, "Do not love the world or anything in the world. If anyone loves the world, love for the Father is not in them."

What is the implication of the love of the Father not being in me? It means I like it here, and I'd better enjoy it while it lasts because things will never get better than this place for me.

God has never been interested in being one among competing suitors.

Do you remember the story of Lot, who was warned by God to leave Sodom because of the destruction coming to that city? Lot's wife couldn't bear the thought of leaving. Her heart was tied to the city. She loved it and all it had to offer. The Bible says she turned to look upon the city—a gaze that spoke of where her true desires lay—and came under the wrath of God, becoming a pillar of salt. The love of the Father was not in her. She loved the world and the things it had to offer and became God's enemy.

How do you feel about a married guy who sleeps around on his wife? Hang with me, this is related.

How about it . . . what do you think of the guy who sleeps around? Would you have anything to do with him? Would you overlook the behavior as no big deal? Of course you wouldn't. All good people want to remove themselves from someone who values others so little. We want to stay away from those people.

But let's make sure this doesn't make us all hypocrites.

This is why we need to drill down on where our true yearnings lie, because if we love the world, if we are "a friend" of the world, God has a word to describe us: adulterer. God looks at his children who love the world and the stuff in it as "sleeping around"—looking to get their thrills from someone other than him. But God takes it a step further. He's not content to leave our loving this world and the things in it at "adultery."

James 4:4 says, "You adulterous people, don't you know that friendship with the world means enmity against God? Therefore, anyone who chooses to be a friend of the world becomes an enemy of God."

God says that if we love the world, we are not just adulterers but his enemies, which is really rotten because now, where there was one, we have two enemies: the world and God!

If you look at it as a math equation, it's pretty straightforward—a simple question with an easy answer. Let's see . . . friend of the world or friend of God? . . . I pick God! But God knew it wouldn't be that easy, that the Enemy would be working overtime, tempting us to see how close we can get in bed with the world without getting burned.

That's why we had to be warned of something that seems so simple: don't love the world or what's in it.

Do you want to do things God's way? Do you want to avoid being his enemy? Then ask yourself: Do I love this world? Do I love the things in this world? Your answer matters.

———

THIRD STEP TO A SURRENDERED LIFE: Know where your struggles come from (devil, world).

Action Step

Take some time to think about what you would do to keep you off track if you were the devil. What fears and thoughts would most derail you from the peace available to you in Christ? Be honest about what you truly live for. Identify at least three things that compete with God for the top spot in your life. Ask yourself, am I a lover of this world?

Prayer

God, please help me love you more than anything else in this world. Please also help me remember that the devil is real and he hates me as he hates you. The presence of your Spirit and the hope of heaven are far greater than anything I can find apart from you. Help me understand that I truly am a stranger in this land.

We're naturally inclined to like/love the world and what's in it because of our third enemy.

Three

Where Our Struggles Really Come From (Part 2)

WHAT IS THE THIRD ENEMY?

That guy in the mirror: me.

Or how the Bible puts it: the flesh.

Our flesh is so powerful. Remember the guy at the softball game in the beginning of the last chapter? Yeah, that guy. It was merely a story about my flesh being given the reins of my life for a while. I brought that on myself. It didn't "happen" to me. I'm not a victim and neither are you. We make choices and we must recognize our freedom to make right choices . . . and to choose to walk uprightly.

My example of getting into a major league argument with the umpire of a Little League game (in front of the parents, ugh!) might lead you to say, "Okay, fine, but that's nothing compared to what I've done."

Two things: First, for the record, this is by no means the

worst sin I've ever committed in my life; and second, it doesn't matter one bit. Whether you're the pastor or the worst felon, if you've come to Jesus, you've been radically saved and so have I. And it doesn't matter who you were or what you've done. There isn't a person alive who hasn't done, hasn't thought of doing, or isn't capable of doing in the flesh any- and everything you have done, have thought of doing, or are capable of doing—and that goes for me too. My flesh is not different from your flesh.

Truth is, my flesh craves filth. I love filth . . . in my flesh.

———

Mark stared down at his Thai food, much quieter than normal. I looked across the small table, wondering what happened to the wry sense of humor and ready smile. What was he about to say? After all, it was Mark who had asked me to lunch. A couple of deep breaths later, he glanced up and across the table. After a moment, he said, "Kevin, I have something to tell you. I've been smoking heroin with a friend."

The look on my face couldn't have told him a whole lot. Like I said, I've heard it all. "You can smoke heroin?"

"Do you hate me? Do you want to leave?"

"No, Mark, of course I don't hate you. And no, I don't want to leave."

"I can't believe I let myself do it. I don't know why I would even go there. I don't know how it even happened. What's wrong with me? I'm such a total loser."

Mark has genuinely repented and hasn't touched the stuff

since, but in the moment, he just couldn't understand why he would fall so far so fast. The fact is, you're not much different from Mark. Neither am I. Oh, maybe you're not smoking heroine or shooting meth, but how about that other sin—the one that gets you every time? If we're honest with ourselves, every one of us is a sinner. Let's be honest, it's practically our middle name.

Rob didn't want to talk about what his flesh was up to when no one was looking—at least when he thought no one was looking. In moments away from the sin, drowning in feelings of personal disgust, he convinced himself that none of his other friends (all professing Christians) would ever stoop so low. So he kept it to himself and kept right on doing it, until the day he got caught when he was in his late thirties. It was all so vile. No one struggled like he did, he told himself, giving power to his enemy.

Or take Carol . . .

"Hey, it's not that big of a deal," she told herself while continuing to thumb through the magazine at the salon, lingering over the male model photographs, letting her mind wander a bit. Okay, sure, it was technically sin, but it wasn't actually that bad, was it? Surely not something she needed to talk about . . . That would be embarrassing. None of her friends were drawn to this kind of thing . . . were they?

As fiercely as the spiritual war rages all around me, the battle is every bit as fierce within me, and the outcome as consequential. My flesh has no interest in giving up. How about yours?

My flesh is at war—at war with God and with my spirit, just as is the devil and the world, and for the exact same reason:

total control. My flesh is not interested in relinquishing control. It screams defiance at any threat to its liberty. My flesh is determined to remain majority owner in this company called ME. There is nothing more natural, more comfortable, more familiar than feeding the flesh.

We don't get to be couch-potato Christians—merely saying what we believe and then letting Jesus do the rest as we go back to the Internet. Our flesh, our inclinations and physical body, is playing for the other team, for the dark side. And Scripture warns us repeatedly to be vigilant against the desires of the flesh, to flee from youthful lusts and give no opportunity to the flesh, which implies something particular about me and what I need to do in the face of these enemies.

If I'm fleeing and giving no opportunity to my flesh, I'm doing something and going somewhere. Let's not believe the deceit that we have nothing to do after coming to Christ.

The fact is that we must defeat the inclinations of our flesh. That which is defeating us must itself be defeated by choosing to ignore these unhealthy inclinations, choosing instead to do what the Bible tells us is right. This is what I call a beautiful defeat.

Three against one—doesn't sound like a fair fight, does it? And it won't end well if we insist on ignoring what the Scriptures say. Spiritual battles (struggles of every kind) fought God's way turn out very well. The same battles, taken in our own strength—not so well. War is serious business.

The big lie whispered incessantly by the Enemy is that only you struggle, only you are the vile one. But remember the apostle Paul's declaration that he was the chief of sinners (1 Tim. 1:15 KJV)? We tend to discount that, telling ourselves, well, he really wasn't all that bad, certainly not as bad as I am. The reason super-apostle Paul could say this is because he wasn't looking across the street to his neighbor and drawing a comparison. He was looking in the mirror—at himself in light of the righteousness of God's law, the Big Ten—and against that standard, he was utterly corrupt. You and I are no different from Paul. He was the chief of sinners . . . and so am I . . . and so are you.

The fact is, when it comes to sinning, there aren't any bottom-rung tribe members. Everyone's a chief.

To make sure no one comes away from the discussion thinking they are better (or worse) than the next person, we get a little clarity from the book of Romans. Paul spends some time at the beginning of that book recounting how bad the Gentiles (non-Jews) are. And just when it is easy to imagine the Jews thinking they have a moral leg up on everyone else, he turns to them and makes the point that from God's perspective, outside of Jesus Christ, every Jew is just as bad as the worst Gentile.

The salient point is that we're all in the same boat and it's sinking. In a paraphrase of Romans 3:9–18, Paul explained it like this:

> Are we (the Jews) better than the Gentiles? No. We have proved that everyone is under sin—as it is written (in the Old Testament). There isn't one righteous person, not one. No one understands. No one seeks after God. . . . Their throat

is an open grave. They use deceit; the poison of snakes is under their lips, whose mouth is full of cursing and bitterness; with their feet they are swift to shed blood. . . . There is no fear of God before their eyes.

If I think I'm better than others because I don't go to the same extent or sin in the same way they do, then I'd better think again. If I think I've sinned so badly that God couldn't possibly love me, God says, *No, there's nothing unique about your sin. You're the same as everyone else*—all sin separates from God.

Now that we know where we stand before God, how do we get up and move on from where we are? Do we just need to try a little harder, grab the steering wheel of life a little firmer, until our knuckles turn white (again)?

Remember, God isn't as interested in what you did as in what you choose to do next.

If you're in the pigsty, get up and go home. The Father knows where you've been. He knows what you've done. And he's still waiting for you with open arms. But the next step, the one you take when the sun rises, needs to come from a different place than your determination to be a better Christian.

Let's first remember that his love never fails and his mercies are new every morning (Lam. 3:22–23)! That's fantastic news. Think for a moment of the worst sin you've committed . . . Yeah, that one. If you're like most people, your mind raced with lightning speed to that moment you wish you could take back and relive. What's more, the thought didn't come alone. Along with it came a wagonload of guilt that builds pressure in your chest like a trapped hot-air balloon every time those memories surface. Is there true forgiveness for these things? Truth is, you just can't forgive yourself because God doesn't really forgive and forget for that sort of thing, does he?

One of the biggest problems with our thoughts of God is that we can't quite shake the idea that he's like us, only bigger. Most of us spend little time thinking about the god we've created in our own image; we just take it for granted that our vague idea of him is accurate. Because we tend to think carelessly about God—that he's like us—we come to believe a lie that even though we've confessed our sin, we aren't fully forgiven (because we don't forgive so easily). Why else would that wave of guilt rise up every time memory serves to taunt us with the blackness of our failures?

If you were really forgiven, wouldn't you feel it?

Feelings are a lot like the wind—powerful, but they come and go. We'd better find something more reliable to base our understanding on than how we may be feeling in any given moment.

"A broken and contrite heart you, God, will not despise," says Psalm 51:17, and in Psalm 34, we are told that God is near those who have a broken heart and saves those who have a contrite spirit.

Is your heart broken over your sin? Do you come to the Father with a heart crushed from the sin you've committed against him, yourself, and others? Are you like the man Jesus saw weeping in the temple, too ashamed to lift his eyes to heaven, beating his chest, crying out, "God, have mercy on me, a sinner" (Luke 18:13)?

The merciful, gentle Father comes near to you whose heart is broken over sin, whose spirit is crushed under the guilt and grief of sin.

God is near. He's a God of mercy, but he is also a God of justice. At first glance, this might seem like the bad news. *He's a God of justice? After what I've done, no wonder I don't feel forgiven.* But the exact opposite is true if we come to God his way. Too often, we'd rather come to God on our terms rather than his . . . like Cain in the Old Testament.

Perhaps everyone knows the story of Adam and Eve's sons, Cain and Abel. From the narrative, we infer that God had made clear to the young men his requirements for sacrificing to him. Abel brought to God a blood sacrifice, while Cain brought to God of the produce of his gardening/farming efforts. God received Abel's sacrifice (who had come to God on God's terms) but rejected Cain's (who came to God on his own terms).

The Bible doesn't speak of Cain's intentions, the quality of the produce he brought, or the reverence with which he offered it to God. Cain was a man of the soil. I've never met a farmer who didn't care deeply about the quality of the fruit, grain, or vegetables he produced. It's possible Cain used his gifts to bring his very best to God. His intentions seemed so good, but the day didn't end so well for him. His sacrifice, his gifts, his offering to God—all of it—was completely rejected. It seems so harsh.

We're too much like Cain, determined to approach God in a manner we deem appropriate. But when it comes to forgiveness for sins, God says, in effect, *I want it done my way.*

And what is that way? Where do the broken and contrite

go? Where does the weak and wounded sinner find true forgiveness? Jesus says, "Come to me, all you who are weary and burdened, and I will give you rest" (Matt. 11:28).

But some may protest that they just can't seem to find the "rest" spoken of. Maybe you have come to the cross and confessed your sins but still don't feel forgiven. Don't settle for how you might be feeling just now. It's time to put feelings in their place—time to get proactive about what the Bible says has happened and what we are told we must now do.

God being a God of justice is not the bad news for us sinners; it's the great news. It is because of the justice of God that we are truly forgiven. That's what God is trying to tell us in 1 John 1:9: "If we confess our sins, he is faithful *and just* and will forgive us our sins and purify us from all unrighteousness" (emphasis added).

We are told here that if we confess, God is faithful to forgive. This simply means that he will do exactly what he says he will do. He can be trusted to follow through. There's no "maybe" or "perhaps" with God when it comes to forgiving our confessed sins. He is faithful to do so, but he isn't just faithful. He's also just. He is the God of justice and when we truly confess, there is a judicial proceeding that is set in motion. Justice is served. Said in reverse, if God didn't forgive you when you confess your sins, he would be unjust.

The Good Judge

The Bible says that God's wrath is coming on the entire world. But this is out of step with the God that Americans, by an overwhelming majority, say they believe in. How can the God who is love bring wrath and punishment? Who wants that God around?

God's wrath is coming *because* he is the God of love, not *in spite of* being the God of love. You see, he's a good judge. Someone recently explained it like this: If you're standing in front of a judge, accusing the murderer who killed your best friend in cold blood, you wouldn't want the judge to release him. If he let the murderer go free, you'd say he was a bad judge. Good and loving judges punish evildoers. This is why we can be confident that God is good. Evil will be punished. Someday. Payday.

In Jesus Christ, the sins of the whole world have been accounted for. First John 2:2 says, "And he is the propitiation for our sins: and not for ours only, but also for the sins of the whole world" (KJV).

That word *propitiation* is an interesting one. It means appeasement—that the wrath of God was appeased in the death of Jesus Christ. When you stand before the good, loving, just Judge and confess your guilt, he cleanses you from all unrighteousness because justice must be served, and the price has already been paid—the debt has been collected. Though you are free to go, recognize the liberty you now have is the liberty to walk in obedience to the Word.

How do our feelings of past sin enter into the equation? At this point, we have a choice to make. Are we "victim" or "victor"? We can walk in the defeat of past sins based on feelings, or we can believe what God has said: you have been cleansed from all unrighteousness. You serve a just, good, and loving God. *You're clean. How you may be feeling has no relevance against what God has said.* Choose to believe God instead of your feelings. When I'm struggling against the temptation to beat myself up for things God has already forgiven, I repeat the words of God in my mind, the verses that contain his message to me.

Say No to Guilt

The apostle Paul offers good advice in Philippians 3:13 where he says (my paraphrase), "I don't consider that I've already arrived but here is what I do. I forget those things that are in my past and focus on my future in Christ Jesus."

This is the guy who was complicit in many state-sponsored incarcerations and murders of Christians. Think his conscience didn't torment him from time to time? Paul was a real person who had to discipline his mind to be filled with thoughts of the future God had called him to. We need to do the same. We need to say no to guilt.

But how?

First off, let's recognize that for the forgiven, guilt over past sin is not an emotion that comes from the Holy Spirit. If guilt rises up to torment, it isn't from God. The deceiver wants you and me to wallow in the cesspool of guilt over past (but forgiven) sin. It's one of his best tricks, distracting Christians from the life God intends by relentless guilt over that which has already been paid for. Feelings of guilt over forgiven sin are from the enemy, which Ephesians 6:12 makes clear. We're not just wrestling within ourselves. This fight (a struggle, a war) is against principalities, powers, and spiritual wickedness in high places.

The next time the Enemy wants to take you down with guilt over forgiven sin, take every thought captive to the lordship of Jesus Christ. In other words, be so familiar with what the Bible says about your forgiveness that whatever you are experiencing may not be viewed in a manner contradictive to what you know to be true. When guilt rears its disfigured head, immediately say, "I take that thought captive to the lordship of Jesus Christ." Why say it out loud? The Enemy can't read your thoughts but he can hear you. Let him hear, every time he tempts you with guilt, your bold calling on the name of Jesus. The last thing Satan wants is for his efforts at destroying you through the dirtiness of guilt to result in you coming to the one who has already won the victory. Resist the devil and he will flee (James 4:7).

Choose to believe the truth. You're clean. You're free.

THIRD STEP TO A SURRENDERED LIFE: Know where your struggles come from (the flesh).

Action Step

Identify the emotions (e.g., anger, lust, fear) that tend to invade your spirit. What are the people, places, or things that tend to precede you being someone other than who you want to be? As you begin to identify these things, also begin to plan in advance how you will choose another course when they enter into your life in the future.

Prayer

God, please help me see my true enemies in my daily living. Make me aware of the devil and his lies, help me live for more than what this world has to offer, and help me be guided by your Spirit and not my flesh. I know that if I am living my life on autopilot none of this will occur. Help me set aside time each morning to talk to you and hear from you both in prayer and in your Word. Please help me not only to be ready to battle but to be fighting the correct opponent in each moment of my life.

Four

Life *with* Your Struggles

OUR LIMITED IMAGINATION ABOUT GOD CAUSES us to miss his awesome way of working in the very midst of our messes. As we've just seen, we face some very real and powerful enemies. I want you to catch a vision of the kind of God whose plan never involves sidestepping who and where you are. The world, the flesh, and the devil don't really want you to catch this vision—which is the reason why you must.

For most of us, the struggles of life seem like random acts of chaos—one disconnected trauma bleeding into the next.

Your messes never look like they have a purpose. But you serve a great God. When I was an assistant coach for my son's fifth-grade basketball team, I got to know Jim, the team's head coach, pretty well. He's easy to be around . . . the kind of guy you can talk to for hours about sports and other "guy" things. Over time, I have come to consider him a friend and greatly enjoy his company.

For some time, my thoughts were filled with a growing

desire to talk to Jim about deeper things. He was aware of the first book I wrote and he knew me to be a Christian. I prayed and asked God to give me an opportunity to talk to Jim about faith. Since I was a committed believer, praying to God about witnessing to a friend, everything would unfold in a godly, spiritual way, right?

Not exactly.

One Tuesday night brought another practice and another new drill from Coach Jim, designed to teach the less aggressive, less confident second-team kids how to get open and be ready to receive a pass in the intensity of a game. The plan was straightforward: put all of the second-team kids on offense and have the first-team kids guard them, with one exception—the first-team point guard. He was given the nearly impossible task of passing the ball to the second-team players who did not yet know how to get open. To make this challenge certifiably impossible, it was decided the point guard would be guarded by the best player on the team, who decided to guard him by getting as close to him as two human beings can get and still be called two people.

Oh . . . and did I mention who was the first-team point guard chosen for this exercise? It was Aaron . . . my son.

Somehow, at this point, I wasn't focused so much on witnessing to Jim about Jesus. Go figure.

As the drill began, the second-team kids just could not get themselves open and the boy guarding Aaron was aggressively waving his hands in Aaron's face as if the NBA championship depended on it. *Give him a break!* I was screaming in my mind

toward the boy. *Think about who Aaron is trying to help improve.*
Pass after pass landed out of bounds or directly in the hands of
the defense. The predictable outcome took its toll. With every
"bad" pass, Aaron's head hung a little lower and his shoulders
stooped in unison with his defeated spirit.

The drill continued. So did the same results.

The boy guarding Aaron couldn't resist a little taunting,
telling Aaron he would never get the ball to his teammates.
As Aaron's head hung lower, my steam meter (not that I was
paying attention to it at the time) was getting dangerously
close to the red line. What parent likes to sit helplessly watching the systematic humiliation of his kid? But I'm not the kind
of dad who rescues his kids from life's challenges, so even
though I was the assistant coach, I didn't say anything . . . out
loud at least.

Inwardly, though, I only screamed louder: *Will Coach Jim
ever end this drill?* It was time for me to leave the gym before,
well, you get the picture. I just couldn't take watching my son
be humiliated further, so I went out into the hallway to cool off
at the drinking fountain. Did my mind immediately think of a
Scripture verse? Did I start humming my favorite worship song?

Not exactly.

I walked outside to my car and pretended to do something,
but I was just getting angrier, so I figured I may as well head
back inside—not exactly logical, I know. As I came through the
front door of the school where we were practicing, three kids
were frantically running toward me yelling, "Coach, Coach,
Aaron is hurt." I raced into the gym where Aaron lay on the

floor crying and grasping his ankle but still talking about how bad he was in the drill and what a bad situation it was for him.

I had had enough. Thirty minutes remained in the practice, but not for us. I helped Aaron to his feet and told him to get dressed. We were going home.

Remember that part about witnessing for Jesus?

While Aaron got dressed I walked over to the coach and yelled at him in front of all the kids. I told him that if he wanted to hurt my son, he could have had him go over to the wall and bang his head repeatedly. I finished my verbal explosion by telling Jim that this was a bunch of @%$#**.

Aaron and I walked quickly to the car on this cold winter night. We got in, shut the door, and turned on the engine to get some heat.

"Hey, son, are you okay?" I asked.

We sat there in the car not saying anything for what seemed like five minutes. Finally, Aaron spoke. "What do we do now?"

Total blank.

I had no idea what to do. What do you do when you screw up . . . bad? Remember, I'm the Christian dad. Why did I yell at the very person I had asked God to give me an opportunity to share the gospel with? After what I had just done, the idea of getting face-to-face with Jim to tell him about the love of Jesus was ludicrous.

We did not want to go back into practice and we did not want to go home. Maybe we could drown out our negative feelings by stopping by our favorite place to get wings. We ate in silence until Aaron began sharing his feelings of helplessness and humiliation. I knew what I had done wasn't right, but hearing the pain pour out of my son made my blood boil again.

He wondered if he could ever be a leader on his team and then asked if I thought he could even still play on the team.

I had no answers.

As we got up to leave, I couldn't find my coat. Did I leave it in the car? After a quick check, I realized it was back at the gym. It was a cold night, so I wanted my coat, but there was no way I wanted to go back into that gym. After a few moments of deliberation, I swallowed my pride (a little) and drove back to the school. A wave of relief passed through my chest when we found the place empty and locked up for the night. By now, the anger was being overtaken by feelings of embarrassment and the humiliation I had brought upon myself.

Suddenly, I remembered there had been some praise and worship going on at our church around eight o'clock each night the past couple of weeks. I asked Aaron if he wanted to see what was happening there and he said, "Sure." When we walked into the sanctuary there were people up on the stage playing instruments and singing with a few others scattered throughout the room. We sat in the back row. My mind was spinning with questions, with anger, and with, *If only* . . .

The longer we sat, the more my mind slowed down until I actually felt a measure of calm, although I left the active praise and worship to others. I didn't sing any words. I really didn't do anything except get into the presence of God through the worship of others. You might call it "parasitic worship."

I still did not have any answers, but I did feel a little peace.

I then remembered that my son was with me and had been forced to sit in the back of a church for thirty minutes.

"Are you ready to go?" I asked.

"Sure."

"Have you been bored this whole time?"

"No, Daddy. Isn't it amazing how you can sit and worship God and even though nothing changes about your situation you can feel a lot better?"

A smile of agreement somehow found its way across my face, and I had to chuckle inside while looking down at my young theologian. Nothing had changed but I did feel better, as if God was telling me that none of this was a surprise to him.

The next morning, thoughts of how to retrieve my coat and avoid Jim at the same time occupied my mind. The prospect of facing him didn't do anything for my appetite. Why didn't I just hang a big sign around my neck: "Hi, I'm the guy who calls himself a Christian and doesn't hesitate to publicly cuss at the guy he hopes to tell about his faith"? By now, I was having a bare-knuckle fistfight with myself and feeling pretty low.

Off to the school, but a quick check in the gym and the lost-and-found left me empty-handed. One option remained: Jim had the coat and I would have to go by his store and pick it up. Great—the worst of all possible options.

Reluctantly, I headed for his store, but just before I turned right into his parking lot, a great idea presented itself. *Why not turn left instead and go to the coffee shop across the street?* Trust me, it seemed very logical at the time. I was still too angry to talk to him. All I could think about were all the things he did wrong, although I did have a fairly good sense that he would never do anything to intentionally bring any sort of harm to my son. In the moment, though, it was easy to constantly push that thought to the corners of my mind and focus on all the bad things he did to humiliate my son, get him injured, and bring on my anger.

Ever notice how hard it is to cool off? It gets even harder when we are unwilling to take responsibility for our own behavior. Sometimes when we're deeply embarrassed, we push back harder to deflect the attention away from ourselves and toward the person we have actually wronged. That morning, I just didn't think I could be kind. Besides, the chair in the coffee shop was really comfortable. I drank my coffee and talked to God about the situation, but frankly, sometimes he just doesn't care much about how comfortable we are . . . especially when we need to surrender to him and his purposes.

As if on cue, the door to the coffee shop opened and in walked Jim with a smile on his face and my coat in his hand.

"Isn't it a little cold to go without a coat?"

"Hey, thanks," I said, just before the dead air settled between us.

Silence.

Jim turned to leave but hesitated as he stood holding the opened door.

"Do you want to talk?"

(That's what Jim said. What the Holy Spirit said was, *Do you want to surrender to me?*)

My first thought was, *Yeah, I want to talk . . . to someone else!*

But instead I replied, "I guess," and he sat down directly across the table from me.

As I sat there brooding about how angry I was and how I had humiliated myself and tarnished my testimony, almost involuntarily my mouth spoke the words, "Please forgive me."

My mouth and mind were then instantly at war. I remember thinking, *Forgive me? For what?*

"Kevin, you do not need to ask me for forgiveness," Jim responded in a conciliatory tone.

But my mouth (heart/Holy Spirit) went on without my approval as I said, "I appreciate that, Jim, but I do need to ask for your forgiveness as my God requires it and so do I, based on my faith in God. It is not acceptable for me to treat you that way while at the same time claiming to be a follower of Jesus."

By God's grace, I was forgiven and—this is the awesome thing about our grace-filled God—if we humble ourselves and let him, he will use the very messes we find ourselves in to accomplish his purposes. Jim now knew what I valued as a Christian (though I wish I had embodied it better!) and—crucially—the door was not shut to future sharing and openness.

A choice faces us every time we are in a mess, entrapped in sin, or confronting our enemy in the world: Will I believe that God can find me here and find a way forward *in* the mess or will I harden my heart, protect my pride, and simply wish I were somewhere else?

Keep yourself open to some amazing possibilities.

No question, Satan is at work trying to destroy, but God is at work too. He has an alternative purpose in the worst things we face. He's a specialist at taking the darkest day and turning it into something beautiful in your life.

This is exactly what the Bible is all about. God is a savior—the Savior. Most times his salvation takes a path we didn't anticipate, and almost always it's through, not around, our problems . . . and only when we yield our hearts and surrender our wills to him.

We've all had what might be referred to as a "Red Sea" moment—our backs against the wall, where every option seems to lead to disaster—but how about the real thing? Several million people without any ability to defend themselves and the army of Pharaoh bearing down on them with one purpose: slaughter. The Red Sea stood to their backs like a prison wall. There was nothing to do but wait for the inevitable. The people cried out against Moses, and Moses cried out to God for mercy, for help, for salvation.

How big are your problems? Impossible? Insurmountable? A complete disaster? Gut-wrenchingly hard? This isn't necessarily the bad news. When the scale of our troubles is beyond our abilities to do anything about them, God has the perfect opportunity to teach us something important. It's as if God allows the trauma to escalate until we are forced to rely on him. When God is our only answer, we are right where he wants us.

And, again, remember his path is almost always through the trouble, through the bitter circumstances, through the impossible relationship, through the deep water, not the easy path around our troubles . . . just like it was for the Israelites.

God opened the sea before his chosen people and they walked through the midst of the waters, on the sea bed, to the other side. This is what God will do for you and for me, if we let him. Without fail, God will take our struggles, our problems, our trials and make them the place where he does his work—we just need to be open to it. This is the powerful and important message of Romans 8:28: "And we know that in all things God works for the good of those who love him, who have been called according to his purpose."

Did you catch that—"all things"? That includes the worst stuff your life has dished up to you, including the worst circumstances you've gotten yourself into. God says those things will work together for good. It's hard to accept, but will you believe what God is saying here? Will you give him your worst and let him make something good out of it? He will manifest his power in the middle of your mess. It's not about desiring to get away from your circumstances but drawing near to God in the middle of them.

When we come to the place where we are willing to give God our struggles, burdens, trials, messes, it's a place of great release. Have you ever been under water for too long and then finally made it to the surface? Surrendering to God is like that, and he wants us to breathe in the life-giving air. I'm guessing it's a lot like the Israelites felt when they made it to the other side of the Red Sea.

But God didn't want them to stop their journey. They still had a long way to go . . . and so do you and I.

God never covers us with his mercy only to leave us. It's

just one stop on the journey—a great place to rest and get our bearings—but he has something more for you and me.

And everything in us is going to resist it because, humanly speaking, it's unnatural, ugly even. But when we see this step through the eyes of the Spirit, something that was at first repulsive becomes a thing of breathtaking beauty.

FOURTH STEP TO A SURRENDERED LIFE: Determine to live through your struggles rather than around them.

Action Step

Try not to eliminate struggle, but ask God to help you discover his purpose in it.

Prayer

Lord, please forgive me for constantly running from you at the times when I need you most. Remind me of the times you have rescued me in the past. Thank you for showing me in the Bible where you did the same for your people. Help me realize that all life events are not about me and that there is much going on that I do not understand or even see. Most importantly, God, please help me remember that when you say all things will work together you are talking about your perfect plan for eternity and not my immediate need for comfort. Thank you for including me in your plans, and give me wisdom and insight so that I can play my role as you have designed it for me.

God wants to fully release his power in your life. This next step is the path to God's power, but like everything else in the Christian life, it's going to seem upside down and backward. It doesn't sound pretty or inviting, but nothing is more beautiful. Are you ready for the beauty God has for you? Just turn the page.

Part II

A CALL FOR SURRENDER

Five

Just Die

I WANT TO SHARE WITH YOU THE MOST challenging teaching in the entire Bible. It's challenging because like almost everything in the teachings of Jesus, we're called to take action, but it's all upside down and backward—it makes no sense, at least to our flesh. And this particular teaching is unfamiliar territory. You might call it the forgotten teaching of the New Testament.

You won't hear it in any of the many church gatherings around the country trying to get as many people as possible through the front door with concert-quality worship bands and by telling people that God is great with you staying right where he found you. The "nothing but love and grace" crowd isn't much interested in this teaching . . . which is tragic because it is *the central teaching of the Christian life*. But it's not as fun as that sounds and it certainly isn't the easy path, because it has a lot to do with something that all sane people spend their lives trying to avoid.

Death.

And who likes that?

We're uncomfortable with it at the best of times and never ready for it when it knocks on life's door.

My friend thought he was ready to look death in the face—the death of his father. He had been there so many times before: all the ambulance rides, the multiple heart surgeries, the death vigils that never ended in death. He thought he had seen it all, experienced every emotion, so even if he fell apart in the past, this time, clearly the last, he was ready. He had already grieved twice before. I'll let him tell his story . . . about saying good-bye.

––––––––

You know you've spent a lot of time in a hospital when you're on a first-name basis with the guy in the lobby playing the grand piano. After being to the hospital nearly enough times to have a wing named after me, I thought I was ready to face it this time. "Hey, bro," I said to my brother over the phone, "you better get here quickly. Without saying it, the doc has indicated to me that Dad isn't going to make it this time." I had the emotions under control and well regulated. I'd been here many times before in this eighteen-year pilgrimage. I knew what it was about. I had already grieved the last time. This was not unexpected.

Over the course of the next hours, one by one, family began to arrive. Before long the surgeon rounded the corner into the waiting room and with all the sensitivity of a squid blurted out,

"If you have anything you want to say, now is the time. I don't know how this is going to turn out." The deadpan tone and clipped instruction suggested he had no confidence Dad would make it through the emergency surgery this time. *You can hardly blame him,* I told myself. Death is as common to him as the setting sun. Still, in some way, I sensed that dignity had suffered a blow. This was my dad we were talking about, after all.

Without speaking we all shuffled down the hallway to his room. What was I going to say? *No worries, I've been here before, this is perfectly natural.* But when we arrived and surrounded the bed, the solemnity of the moment silenced everyone . . . until Dad began to speak.

"I have something I need to say to you all . . . something I want to tell you."

Glances were exchanged. Instinctively, we all drew in a little closer. What was he going to say?

His eyes moved from Mom, to my sisters, to my brother, to my wife, and then rested on me.

"There's something you need to know, John."

"Yes?" I said nervously.

"Son, you're adopted."

And with that, we all erupted in hysterics. I'm not adopted, okay. Leave it to Dad to take a hallowed moment and crack a joke.

So why were we all now wiping our eyes?

Dad then turned to Mom, slipping his big hand around her strong but small fingers . . . "I love you, Cheryl. You've been a good wife to me."

Mom began to cry in her discreet way, but something caught me off guard. I was getting a little choked up too. I had thought my emotions had been put in a box and tucked away somewhere safe.

He had something for everyone as he went from person to person, but then he looked directly at my brother and me. "I don't think I'm gonna make it this time, boys. Take care of your mother."

I had a firm grip on the bed rails, which was a good thing because my shoulders began to heave. I just couldn't hold it back—like a flash flood suddenly appearing from somewhere in the distant mountains.

"I don't want you to go, Dad," I cried.

"Son, let me go. You've got to let me go."

The sobs came like an avalanche. The ache in my heart at the thought of never seeing Dad again went into overdrive. Let go? I couldn't. I didn't want to. I wasn't ready. The time wasn't right. And yet, in seconds, he was whisked down the hall for the appointment we will all keep but never quite know when to expect.

We were left alone in an empty room. We all fumbled around stupidly for a few awkward moments, then shuffled back to the hospital lobby.

I thought I had Death right where I wanted it—understood, under control, reasonably appraised—and yet, when the moment came, I totally lost it. I think it's because Death is our natural enemy. No matter when he appears, there's always something wrong, something unacceptable, something inappropriate about it—something that violates the essence of who we are. As inevitable as it is, there is always something unnatural about death.

We don't want to die, and yet Jesus said we have to . . . if we're going to be his disciples, his followers. But we don't want to die. It's that simple. We all instinctively hate death. Billions are spent every year to ward off the inevitable. But, ultimately, it's futile. There is a certain kind of ugliness to death that all the amenities of the classiest retirement home or luxury vacation spots for seniors just can't obscure.

———

My friend was sporting at twenty, classy at thirty, dignified at sixty. Though she seemed to live a charmed life, by the time eighty-eight rolled around, all that was gone. Then came the fall, the halting recovery, the convalescent home, and finally, hospice care.

When you walked in, death was the first thing to greet you . . . or should I say, assault you? Even before the smiles of the wonderful caregiver opening the front door with a warm welcome. It wasn't so much a door as a portal to the afterlife, but whatever you called it, once opened, the essence of death, that smell, permeated through all the pine-scented cleaner to leave you with the urgent feeling of needing to get out of there as soon as possible. People talk about the "smell" of death—yeah, I know what they mean. It stinks, literally.

But, technically, she wasn't dead yet. I pushed open the

door to the tiny room she had been occupying for the last leg of the journey. *Four grand a month for this?* I thought to myself. *Unbelievable.* There, on the spare bed against the wall, lay a near rigid frame, so different from a few short months back. Vacant, unblinking eyes stared from the back of her skull, past dehydrated skin turned hard as it pressed against unyielding facial bones. It was hard to keep looking at her. The mouth gaped open, never closing, yet the lungs continued to heave as every rattling, labored breath expelled foul, death-corrupted air into the room.

You can put lipstick on a corpse, but you can't make death look pretty.

Death—it's the mortal enemy of our flesh.

I hate death.

Which is the core problem at the center of it all, because death is exactly what Jesus wants for you and me. That's right—death. It is the central teaching of the life of a disciple. Without death, nothing else can happen.

Jesus wants to love you to death, literally.

"Wait a minute . . . Jesus was here to deliver—to give us a full, rich life—to accept us and save us regardless of what we do?"

Well, yes . . . and no. And it's the "no" part that Christians usually miss by a wide margin, just like my friend Julie who recently wrote in her journal (and gave me permission to share) . . .

I'm weary of my schedule, exhausted by my career. My life is passing me by . . . I'm over committed, living in complete and utter worship of idols, numbing my reality with TV, travel, shopping, anything . . . I find myself searching . . . looking for everything but God . . . and yet, I'm searching for God too . . . feeling helpless . . . I have no control of my own life . . . I'm giving lip service to God but running after more and more things that give quick comfort, distract, and fit into what my identity has become: a worshipper at the altar of "My Job Is Important," and "I'm Very Busy."

I've depleted myself physically, mentally, and spiritually. I'm empty. And for what? For what Socrates calls "the barrenness of a busy life." So, what have I become? Prideful, dangerous, conflicted, backslidden, doubtful, confused, disappointed.

Where are the good adjectives?

I'm always asking/begging God for forgiveness, guidance, and blessing, *but* I don't wait upon him. I don't listen. I am not surrendered to him and his will . . . not really.

If I'm honest, I've reached midlife and I literally have no idea—no idea—what God's purpose is for my life. I realize now that I just always assumed that I knew . . . but I don't. I've given birth to a lot of Ishmaels as if God is obligated to bless my many "great ideas" and blistering pace.

I've embraced—no, prostituted myself to—my idol of busyness. "Who is Julie?" "Oh, Julie, she's busy." My idol is more important than people. I've become so frantic and inattentive to people that I often can't fully recall what I've said, decisions I've made.

So, what do I value, really? To hear family, friends, co-workers, and even strangers say, "Wow, Julie is amazing! How does she ever get it all done?"

And I keep bowing down . . . to my idol . . . accomplished, hardworking, amazing, busy Julie.

"Who is Julie?"

"She's busy."

. . . and empty.

Shame . . . it's not something I've thought about much. I've always been too busy for shame . . . but now? Suddenly I'm holding its hand while at the same time, trying to shake loose its grip and get away. Incessantly it whispers to me . . . "You'll never measure up, not to God's standards or the world's or the church's either . . . It's too late for you, Julie."

Are the lies I've told myself now the sum of my life . . . of who I am?

If I am not the busy, scheduled, achieving, people-pleasing mess that leaves little room for God's leading, then who I am is pretty much a mystery to me.

Can I make a different choice? . . . with baby steps . . . make a choice to approach a loving God who might see me as something other than broken and beyond repair?

The problem with Julie . . . the problem with all of us . . . the reason we are still empty even though we have come to faith in Jesus is . . .

We're too alive.

Jesus wants Julie, and you, and me . . . dead.

Death—it looks ugly to us.

But Jesus doesn't care about all that, because the death we fear isn't nearly so ugly as the continued life of our flesh.

He loves you and me so much he wants our enemies dead.

Remember that bit about Jesus' teaching being upside down and backward? This is from the perspective of our flesh, that part of us that isn't yet redeemed. Jesus never tells our flesh what it wants to hear. When it comes to our flesh, he will tell us what we need to do but he won't do it for us.

Dying is antithetical to the survival instinct. But for those of us determined to triumph through our struggles, for those of us who don't want our lives to be an empty claim about the "abundant life," for those of us who know we're missing it, we have to go there because we can no longer take the scream coming from somewhere within our hearts.

And that's why Jesus said, "If any man will come after me, let him deny himself, and take up his cross daily, and follow me" (Luke 9:23 KJV).

But Jesus already died on the cross, so isn't all the dying already done?

No, it isn't.

What "Death" Really Means

What, exactly, was Jesus saying in instructing his disciples (you and me) to take up our cross?

Inevitably, someone will show up pulling a wooden cross across town, across the state, or across the country—taking literally the instruction of Jesus. If that's your gig, good for you, but you can drag a cross the size of a telephone pole from your front door to Antarctica and never get close to the simple teaching Jesus was instructing his true followers to do.

Jesus was saying that if we want to be true followers of him, we have to die. It's that simple. Jesus doesn't want you to be a miserable Christian, which is why he wants you to die. *A cross is the instrument of the death of the flesh.* Every true follower of Jesus needs to keep handy his metaphorical cross because we have to "take up" our cross every day.

Why is it necessary to carry one of these around? First and foremost, because Jesus said to—what more do we need than a direct instruction from our Lord and Savior? Jesus said to take it up, so pick up yours and I'll pick up mine, and let's get going. But God is merciful and offers us a little more explanation in Romans 8:23 as to why it's necessary to carry one of these around: "We . . . groan within ourselves, waiting for the adoption [which is] the redemption of our body" (KJV).

Maybe you noticed the last time you checked—your body isn't redeemed and neither is mine, and neither is the physical world.

Sometimes it's hard to understand why so many bad things happen. Just this week, a tornado in Oklahoma killed more than twenty elementary school children as the building collapsed on top of them, and the country of Syria is being torn to shreds by various warring factions. There's craziness everywhere.

Then there are the difficult things we face personally . . . like our fleshly impulses to engage in things that are dishonoring to God and to our own bodies. Never mind all the wicked things going on in the world and in the lives of other people. Why, if we have given our lives to God and are told in the Word that we are a new creation and the old man has passed away, do we continue to face challenges and temptations? Why does sin look and feel so good? It's not "spiritual" to say so, but it does look good and feels good too, if only for a season. If you're honest with yourself, your flesh craves sin. It's true even of those who lead a surrendered life.

Why is that? Why do I have to struggle against my own after I've surrendered to Jesus Christ?

makes sense that we would be confused on this point. many preachers who teach a kind of post-salvation m, literally telling people that once you have are saved, you don't have to struggle against sin. n't Jesus come to set us free?

n there's Craig's experience, some variation of ll had. Craig had just come off of an amazing trip. eks he had been working with a domestic mis- g inner-city youth escape from the gang culture. oved, lives were changed, and Craig was riding a igh. Then, about three days after getting home, he e bored and tired and logged on to the Internet to e "fail compilations," videos of people doing crazy things and caught in hilarious circumstances. He didn't begin this R & R thinking he was two mouse clicks from hard-core porn, but that's where he wound up.

Craig repented but was bewildered at his own choices and behavior. How was it possible to go from a spiritual high, where God had demonstrably used him in true ministry, to where he wound up? What happened?

The same thing that happens to all of us—we don't take up our cross daily. My flesh needs to be crucified every day. Here's what I do (when I'm on my game and thinking right!).

I begin every day with my body bowed before God. Of course, there is no rule or "right" prayer position, but comple surrender to God is a serious business, which is why m Christians literally bow their heads, get on their knees, prostrate on the floor. You've already seen from my stor I forget this often. I have to do this every day and wh when I walk in my flesh, I pay the consequences— time but, eventually, if I've been neglecting centeri on the God I serve, I and many around me will p

My mind needs to be washed . . . in the water This means opening up my Bible and actually rea my day to God in a simple prayer: "This is yo Please fill me with your Spirit to walk as you w walk today." Remember, the Bible says that if we Spirit, we will not fulfill the desires of the flesh When temptation comes (I didn't say "if" but "wher taken up my cross, I'm ready to withstand what cor

Just like the situation with Craig, struggle im

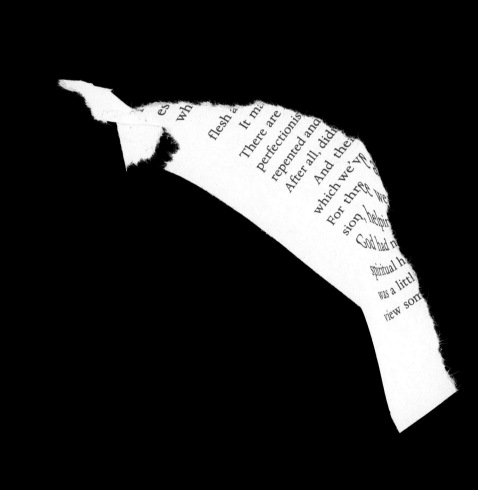

following a "spiritual victory" happens in the Bible as well. Take Elijah, the powerful prophet of God in the Old Testament. God would no longer tolerate the wickedness and influence of the prophets of Baal and called on Elijah to act. So Elijah challenged the prophets of Baal in a contest to prove who was the real all-powerful God: Baal or Yahweh.

Here was the deal he offered the pagan prophets—prepare a bull for sacrifice, put it on the altar, but don't light the fire. Instead, call on the god Baal to light the fire of the altar.

The prophets of Baal were only too eager to take up the challenge. From morning until noon they called out to Baal: nothing. So they jumped on the altar and kept up the yelling until Elijah decided to have a little fun, suggesting that maybe Baal was sleeping, on a journey, or talking to someone else. The prophets of Baal yelled all the louder and began to cut themselves with knives until the blood ran freely over their bodies. Still nothing.

Now it was Elijah's turn. He had an altar built, placed all the wood ready for lighting, prepared the sacrifice, had a trench built around the altar, and then had the whole thing doused with water until everything was drenched and the trench was filled with water too.

Elijah called upon Jehovah, and the entire preparation—stones, wood, bull, even the water—was consumed until nothing remained but ashes.

Elijah then captured the prophets of Baal and killed them all. Victory: *God!*

Now that's a mountaintop experience. Elijah was chosen by God to be the instrument of his power and glory, and ran with it, even taunting and mocking the pagan prophets. After so visible and dramatic an experience of God's power, what could shake his confidence?

But something did.

Baal worshiper Queen Jezebel could smell the winds of rebellion like a buzzard smells the fetid corpse of a dead rat from ten miles. She vowed to hunt Elijah down and kill him. When Elijah got wind of it, did he meet the next challenge with even more confidence in God? No, he didn't. He caved and ran away to hide in the desert. Elijah, powerful prophet of the living God, went from epic victory to colossal failure inside of a few days.

Pathetic, right? Yeah, pathetic . . . just like you . . . and me.

Then there's the apostle Peter—fearless, big, bold, type-A leader. He was ready to face all odds, had a successful ministry as a disciple of Jesus, was present at the transfiguration, and boldly affirmed, "You are the Messiah, the Son of the living God" (Matt. 16:16). Then Jesus declared him to be a rock. It was three-plus years of solid, mountaintop experiences. The blind had been healed, the lame walked, the hungry were fed by the thousands. With such a spiritual pedigree, it's reasonable to expect a life traveling from victory to victory, isn't it?

But Jesus knew Peter's heart—and the heart of all men (including yours and mine)—better than Peter knew it himself.

Upon hearing what was coming, Peter told Jesus he would never leave him—even if everyone else did, he would stand by Jesus' side, to the death if necessary. But after Jesus was arrested, Peter thought he could fulfill his declaration by being an undercover supporter of Jesus, working up the courage to stand near the courtyard fire outside the building where Jesus was being interrogated, but desperately hoping no one would recognize him.

Jesus has never called us to be secretive about our devotion to him. Not then, not now. For the time being, Peter had forgotten what Jesus had taught: "If you deny me before men, I'll deny you before the Father" (Matt. 10:33, author's paraphrase).

Someone began staring . . . Someone knew . . . Someone recognized . . .

Peter's response was to deny knowing the man he had followed for the past few years. How natural for those words to flow from his flesh as the determination to save his life kicked into autopilot.

"No, I'm not from Galilee. I was never with Jesus."

"I've never had anything to do with him."

"I don't even know him!"

Somewhere in the stillness of the night, a rooster began to crow.

When I look at my own life, I have heard that rooster crow too many times. I wish it wasn't so easy to identify with Peter . . . at least the failure part. Why do we tend to go from spiritual high to "autopilot" sin to save ourselves or satisfy our lust when it's so antithetical to who we are . . . to who we've been called to be in Christ?

And, personally, my flesh is too destructive to buy the line of the trendy "I'm a mess, you're a mess, we're all a mess, but God doesn't mind 'cause he's the God of love" church movement.

I know he loves me, but he also said, "Go and sin no more" and "Be holy for I am holy."

In describing his own struggle with the flesh, the apostle Paul cried out, "Who will set me free from the body of this death?" (Rom. 7:24 NASB).

We know the answer is Jesus Christ, but when it comes to a redeemed body of flesh, we get the timing wrong—we think that our spiritual highs should last us for a few years. Try a few minutes. We need to be back on our knees, dying again. Remember the truth about where we live—in a world that is still waiting for redemption.

The following story helped me understand why I need to refocus on God every single, solitary day.

It was more than John had bargained for now that the day of his departure had come. Kintu's fingers were digging into his shoulder blades, clinging desperately to him near the entrance gate to the orphanage. *Why is he leaving without me?* Kintu couldn't understand. He jumped into John's arms and clung desperately to his neck. "Don't leave me. I don't want you to go. You said you are my new father. Take me with you," he pleaded as tears of desperation forced their way through eyes clenched shut against a reality he couldn't change.

It was enough to rip John's heart from his chest, but he forced his emotions down with a hard swallow. John gently took Kintu from his arms and knelt down next to the jeep on the red dirt road, looking directly into his eyes.

"Kintu, *I am* your new father. You are my son. It is settled. You are going to come and live with me in your new home in

Canada. I adopted you, but the paperwork takes about two months. I'll come back for you. I promise."

Kintu's eyes were fixed on John's as fear's heavy breathing refused to subside. Was it really true? Was he truly adopted? Would his father return to get him? Kintu looked warily into John's face, hoping desperately it was true, while still fearing it might not be. How much longer would he have to remain in his bitter life in the orphanage before going home . . . to his new home with his new father? He didn't want to wait. He wanted to go right now but couldn't. How could he trust that his new father would come for him? Would he keep his word?

Feeling Kintu's fear like a thousand knives, John's mind raced for a way to help Kintu trust that he would return. He checked his pockets and did a quick search of his luggage. What could he give? He couldn't come up with anything. John turned, and as he placed his left hand on Kintu's right shoulder, he saw it. After a moment's hesitation, John reached to his left ring finger and pulled off his wedding ring. Taking Kintu's left hand, John slipped the too-big ring onto Kintu's finger. John hadn't planned on his own tears.

"Here, Kintu. This is my wedding ring. Keep it until I return. It is my promise to you that I will come for you."

Like Kintu, we have been given a gift, a ring, a down payment of what is to come. We've been given the Holy Spirit. Right now, we enjoy the Spirit of adoption, as it says in Romans 8:15, "but you received the Spirit of adoption by whom we cry out, 'Abba, Father'" (NKJV).

But our physical bodies are in the same predicament as creation, as Paul continued to explain in verses 22–23, "We know that the whole creation has been groaning as in the pains of childbirth right up to the present time. Not only so, but we ourselves, who have the firstfruits of the Spirit, groan inwardly as we wait eagerly for our adoption to sonship, the redemption of our bodies" (NIV). Our bodies are like Kintu, waiting at the orphanage. We've been adopted. "It is finished!" Jesus cried out from the cross, having paid the debt of our sin in full. But we are waiting for the return of our Redeemer.

This is the reason for the struggle we find within ourselves. Our bodies are not yet redeemed, so we wait, but not without hope. Death has been destroyed. Sin has been dealt a mortal blow. We've been given power over sin. It has no power over us because, despite our sinful bodies, we belong to God and walk by the power of the Spirit, who enables us to walk worthy of our calling (Eph. 4) and to say no to sin.

And this is why we still need a cross, every day.

Our flesh is corrupt; it still craves sin in all its manifestations. We might be saved, but we're still stuck with our flesh . . . for now, at least. It desires things that are inconsistent with a holy life. It chafes against everything that God desires for us. It is our enemy, and that's why *Jesus doesn't just want our flesh subdued—he wants it crucified*. Sinful flesh deserves nothing better than death on a cross. This is why we need to take up our cross *daily*.

We've talked about what this means, practically speaking. We belong to God. We've been redeemed. The power of sin is broken and has no authority over us. When our flesh tempts us to go where we shouldn't—think what must not be dwelt upon, say what shouldn't be said instead of speaking the truth in love—we reject it. We put our flesh on the cross, as it were, and kill it on the spot.

Jesus said "daily," so we get to (need to!) do it over and over again. But that's okay because we're in the battle to triumph over our struggles, to find the abundant life offered by our Lord, and to walk as he walked. We're his disciples, so we get to do what he did. His flesh was crucified. Ours must be as well.

When we put our flesh to death, we find that our struggles and challenges automatically take on a different aspect. We have removed an obstacle to the spiritual success that Jesus wants for us and see our struggles for what God wants of them rather than what our enemy intended. When we say no to our flesh, we are surrendering to another agenda—we're surrendering to what God is doing in our lives and to his use of our struggles to mature us for his purposes and for his glory. As we said in chapter 3, that which is defeating us must itself be defeated by choosing to ignore these unhealthy inclinations and instead to do what the Bible tells us is right.

***

FIFTH STEP TO A SURRENDERED LIFE: Die daily.

Action Step

Make a death certificate for yourself. Be creative and include whatever items make the most sense to you.

Here are some items that are on mine: date of death, cause of death (my choice), do-not-resuscitate order, why I chose for my flesh to die, what I gained in my death.

Prayer

In this moment, God, I commit again to putting my flesh to death. I need more than self-control or more willpower. This is not about avoiding problems. I trust that as my Father, you know what is best for me and I place my trust in your ways rather than my own. Help me continually understand that you will not lead me in a way that is not best for me. Remind me of how well things went when I died on a given day and how wretched I feel about myself when I am driven by out-of-control desires. I know that I will have to do this again tomorrow, God, but let it be said of me today that I died to me and lived for you.

When you arise from this prayer you will be doing nothing less than heading out for battle.

Six

Prepare for Your Mission

ARE WE LIVING A MESS OR ARE WE ON A MISSION?

This question was on my mind when I walked into his office. One look and I knew there had to be a backstory. There was no way this guy could have been a medical doctor his entire life. I don't know exactly what it was. Some might call it the "X" factor, but he was just different, not bad, good in fact, but definitely different. Piercing, alert, intelligent eyes, a strong frame supporting thick yet lithe muscles giving the impression—despite his large size—he was fast as a cat if he wanted to be, along with a commanding manner, all led me to ask what he did prior to medicine.

He was a Navy SEAL! It took me awhile to get it out of him, but it was not surprising if you just looked at him. Figures . . . but kind of ironic too. Here I had been thinking on this issue of daily spiritual warfare, and now I was talking with a Navy SEAL.

"I've never met a SEAL before. It's an honor," I said, sticking out my hand.

"Thanks. The reason you've not met a SEAL before is likely because, except for a few grandstanding ego machines, a SEAL doesn't typically want to be known and there just aren't that many of us around. At any given time, there are only about twenty-five hundred active-duty SEALs."

I was there for an appointment but found myself wanting to pepper him with questions. What could I learn from him about preparation for a mission? A lot, as it turns out. He agreed to answer my questions and we arranged to meet outside the context of the office. But before he would give his final okay, there were a few things I had to agree to.

"Kevin, I'm happy to answer your questions honestly, but you have to agree never to associate my name with any of this—it's critical. I don't mean to be melodramatic, but we [Navy SEALs] never stop having enemies."

Yeah, I know the feeling.

A few days later, he walked into the coffee shop and sat across from me. What he shared with me was harsh and delivered with profanity. I don't condone the rough language, nor some of the practices and behaviors he described (some of which I had to omit)—but I want you to hear his words directly because I was blown away by the fact that I could learn more about my Christian life from a special ops professional soldier than from many a believer trapped in a soft Christian religion.

> It starts with desire, but desire is never enough. You do have to want it, but just because you want to be a SEAL will never carry you to your goal. Lots of people want something. Big

deal. Unless you have the inner grit to never quit, unless the idea of giving up cannot enter your mind, you'll never make it. And believe me, they give you plenty of reasons to quit. Only 20–25 percent make it through BUD/S [Basic Underwater Demolition SEAL Training]. So, a lot try but few make it.

Listening to him, I couldn't help thinking of Jesus' teaching about the narrow and wide ways and about how so few find the narrow way—the way to life. Don't get me wrong, I believe in the unconditional love of God. But the Bible says, "Choose for yourselves this day whom you will serve" (Josh. 24:15). It's all too easy to turn away from the tough path of discipleship.

First thing, Kevin, when thinking of the activity of a SEAL, you need to get rid of the idea of going into battle. That's not what we do. Don't get me wrong. As everyone knows, we're fighters and sometimes we do get into a firefight [not called a gun fight], but when that happens, it's usually because something went wrong. Stealth characterizes our natural mode of operations.

We aren't designed such as infantry battalions that you read about in history books that were used in large-scale attacks (battles) such as D-day or the Battle of the Bulge. We actually end up sucking pretty badly if we get into situations like those where we are greatly outnumbered. Case in point, Operation Red Wings in Afghanistan where we lost four members on the ground and lost another platoon as they were flying in to pull the four out. It was a horrible day in NavSpecWar [Naval Special Warfare], but it was a fight against very large numbers. Don't worry, we made them pay for everything, but I wouldn't ever chalk it up as a win. What the SEAL does is "mission" based. We are masters of unconventional warfare. We operate in small units called platoons—sixteen guys divided into two squads of eight, which are divided into two "fire teams" of four, which are divided into two dive pairs. What we consider a successful mission is one where the enemy doesn't even know we've been there until after we left.

What a powerful image of the Christian life! We may be in a large Christian subculture—but we should really see ourselves as traveling stealthily through enemy territory as we face the world, our own flesh, and the devil. We don't call attention to ourselves, but quietly pray, find strength, and resist temptation.

It all starts with BUD/S. This is the brutal weeding-out process of everyone who would like to become a SEAL. No matter how tough you are coming into the training program, no matter how fit an athlete you are, your weaknesses—mental, physical, emotional—will be discovered and exploited. SEAL instructors are skilled in creating extreme levels of stress to reveal how recruits will respond. You might have been a hero back in your own world, but this program has a way of shredding many more than those who make it through. Typically, only about 20–25 percent of all the recruits make it out of BUD/S. It seems brutal at the time, but the reality is that your life is going to depend on keeping your head in the midst of extreme circumstances. It is through the difficult circumstances that the trainee faces that he exhibits the necessary toughness that will protect him in the field.

Do we really think of the successful Christian life as requiring tough training? Fortunately for us we get a second (and seventh) chance with God—but let's face up to the fact that God wants nothing less than for us to be trained, "a worker who does not need to be ashamed" (2 Tim. 2:15).

What is the worst thing a soldier could do on a mission? There's probably various answers to this, but mine would be this. The worst thing a soldier can do in a firefight is freeze up. . . . He thus becomes a liability and another dynamic that the rest of the squad would have to deal with. There is a 99.99 percent likelihood that this would not happen in a SEAL platoon/squad. Not saying it wouldn't, but highly unlikely.

Hmm. I think sometimes we get so focused on "Jesus and me" that we don't realize that our own struggles affect our brothers and sisters in the faith. Finding a way to keep walking out our mission is critical not only to us but to others. What is the likelihood that we are prepared as people of faith like

SEALs prepare for their jobs? The Bible says that we are to be ready to explain the gospel in season and out of season. Do we prepare so that we are always ready?

> I get scared. Anyone who tells you they don't is full of [it]. I just don't let it stop me; it's what you do with it that sets you apart. You either freeze (panic), or fight/flight. I had a good friend during training. We would go surfing on our time off, go hit the beaches, cruise for chicks. You get the idea. Anyway, we were going through "pool comp" (pool competency for diving), which is a big hurdle for some people because it causes people to panic due to the exercises the instructors make you progress through in the pool. Underwater. Basically they have you at ten feet with scuba tanks, et cetera, on. Then they progressively start tearing things off, wrapping air hoses around your manifold, making knots in them, et cetera. Just to get you to bolt to the surface, a.k.a. panic. Anyway, even though he surfed all the time, was supposedly comfortable in the water, he freaked out and didn't keep his cool. He panicked. My philosophy isn't so much as not to be afraid; it's not to panic. Panic is the killer.

As Christians we have the ultimate reason to not be afraid. But I love how he differentiates panic from fear. When we panic in circumstances is when we start walking in our own counsel, moving further and further away from what God instructs us in his Word (our SEAL training manual!) to do.

There is a huge amount of planning done before a mission begins. Usually the biggest mistakes are getting caught, being seen, or deviating from the plan. But basically, everyone on mission trusts the other person to simply not [mess] up . . . for instance, the raid on Bin Laden's compound. They wanted to get in, kill him, get out. Not get into a long-standing firefight. We're sneaky . . . get in and get the job done. *If* we get caught, detected, the mission would be considered a failure. But again, depends on what the mission is. There is no set mission that SEALs do. Anything and everything from the air to the sea and all in between we've been trained to do. Call us "Jack of all trades, master of none." But masters we are.

Preparation and planning—vital to a successful SEAL mission, but is it any less important to a successful spiritual life behind enemy lines? We've heard it a thousand times: "Put on the whole armor of God, that you may be able to stand against the wiles of the devil" (Eph. 6:11 NKJV). We breeze past Ephesians 6 as if it just isn't that important—as if God doesn't really expect to be taken seriously. We're too focused on a soft kind of Christian religion that wants love without discipleship. That's why we can read Ephesians 6 and yawn. But we need to stop yawning and get enrolled in an even more crucial program than that embraced by the Navy SEALs.

It's more crucial because God wants something more from his true followers. He wants a yielded heart, a willing spirit, and an eager response to his directives. Before we get further into battle prep, let's get real about our true perspective on God and the place he has in our lives. The SEALs clearly understand their chain of command. They know who they answer to and what that person expects of them.

Consultant, Consort, or King?

Do we want a consultant for the life we're striving after, a consort to accompany us along our way, or a King who has total ownership and jurisdiction over every aspect of our lives?

No one has a problem with "Jesus the Consultant." What is a consultant but a guide, a good teacher who gently offers advice and direction? Who doesn't want to hire a good consultant to help get you where you want to go? A good consultant is worth his weight in gold and, best of all, if you don't agree with him and come to an impasse, just show him the door. Consultants don't have the right to hang around, getting in the way of the plans they told you wouldn't work out.

"Jesus the Consultant" is a popular line in our culture because you can give the compliment where no obligation follows. Saying Jesus is a great moral teacher is just another way of saying you're not obligated to do a thing he says. Remember Buddha, Plato, Socrates . . . ? Yeah, we don't have to listen to them either. No "great moral teacher" is authoritative enough to require anyone to do anything he says.

The line goes something like this: Jesus was a great teacher of moral precepts. Really? . . . A great teacher? There isn't one other rational human being in recorded history who came close to saying the crazy things Jesus said.

What are some of the things this "great teacher" had to say?

In Mark 2:5, Jesus told a sick man, "Son, your sins are forgiven." The scribes who overheard this comment didn't fall all over themselves declaring what a great teacher Jesus was. These guys were logical and smart and did the only sensible thing—they took offense at so pretentious and blasphemous a comment. After all, only God has power on earth to forgive sins, right?

In John 8:24, Jesus said, "I told you that you would die in your sins; if you do not believe that I am he, you will indeed die in your sins." Essentially, Jesus was saying that he is the Son of God, and that he and the Father are "one." To die without believing in him as the Messiah is to spend eternity separated from God—not exactly the stuff of a rational mind.

In John 8:56, Jesus said, "Your father Abraham rejoiced at the thought of seeing my day; he saw it and was glad."

The implications of such a claim are ludicrous, which was not lost on the listeners.

In verse 57, they said to him, "You are not yet fifty years old, . . . and you have seen Abraham!" Which is to say, "Give me a break. You expect us to believe what you are saying? It's manifestly false. We know your parents, Mary and Joseph."

Just to make sure he was perfectly clear in what he was saying, Jesus responded, "Before Abraham was born, I am!" (v. 58).

To the Jewish ear, the phrase "I am" had a familiar ring and was a claim of particular meaning. God told Moses (and a whole lot of others throughout the Old Testament) that he was/is the "I am" (the eternally existing One), so to have Jesus claiming not only to have known Abraham but to be "I am" was a little much. So they did the only logical and necessary thing under the circumstances. They picked up rocks to kill Jesus on the spot for claiming to be God.

Good teachers and great philosophers know their limitations. Only lunatics call themselves "God" and expect everyone to believe them. When it comes to being that great teacher, Jesus is, frankly, hard to get along with. Fact is, Jesus just isn't a team player.

- Jesus says, "I am the way and the truth and the life. No one comes to the Father except through me" (John 14:6).
- Jesus claimed to possess all authority in heaven and on earth; therefore, men should obey all his commands (Matt. 28:18, 20).
- We must love him more than we love our closest family members, else we are not worthy of him (Matt. 10:35–38).
- He will come in glory with the angels and reward all men according to their works (Matt. 16:27).
- All nations will be gathered before him, and he will send them into eternal punishment or eternal life (Matt. 25:31–46).

The people who won't let go of the "Jesus as great moral teacher" line rely on their own fertile imaginations rather than on the historical record (the Bible) for the source of their ideas.

If you've styled Jesus as your consultant, you didn't get that idea from the Bible.

Some of us are more comfortable with Jesus as our consort—our companion on this journey we call life. It's comforting to know your companion is always close at hand, walking alongside, ready to respond whenever you call but never obtrusive or overly directive. It's as if we've started on a journey and invited Jesus to come along for the ride. We're going somewhere and we want Jesus to know he's welcome too. That, we tell ourselves, must make him really happy. Jesus likes it when we accept him.

We don't have to step too far back to see who is setting the terms of that relationship. The consort is never in charge. And for some of us, that's just the way we like it. We're good with Jesus as our companion just as long as he doesn't compromise the life we're determined to live.

Everyone who lives as if Jesus is their consultant or their consort is quick to declare that they love Jesus. Sometimes you will hear them referring to Jesus as their copilot. But the real Jesus, the one found in the Bible, isn't interested in being a consultant or a consort to someone else's plans, purposes, and agenda. He's already got that covered:

"If you love me, keep my commands" (John 14:15).

For the self-willed, consultants and consorts are a lot easier to get along with than are kings. Consultants offer services, and consorts offer support to enable you to reach your desired goals. Kings, not so much. Jesus doesn't come offering a smorgasbord of options for how we will take him.

Whether we hire a consultant, seek a consort, or serve a King all depends on our understanding of where we live . . . that's right, where we live. It depends on our citizenship.

For the Christian, the issue is settled. We're citizens of another place. The Bible declares that the world is passing away (1 John 2:17). Our citizenship is in heaven (Phil. 3:20). We are under the leadership and administration of where we are citizens.

Jesus is the King. He's not our consort or consultant to see us through the lives we make for ourselves. He is the King—the King who must be obeyed. But this King is also the gentle Shepherd and the loving Father. He has our very best in mind with every challenge, command, and instruction. When he tells us we need to keep our cross handy, when he tells us to put to death the things our flesh wants to do, he is saying it for our best.

What we are talking about here is a call away from the chaos of a life lived apart from the loving instruction of our King and to the life you and I were meant to have: a life that can only be truly realized after we have surrendered control and have died to ourselves—have literally given up our rights to the life we want and embraced the life God has planned for us.

We're never more effective in this life of challenge and struggle against our spiritual enemies than when we are truly dead to ourselves and the truth of Galatians 2:20 is manifesting itself through us: "I have been crucified with Christ and I no longer live, but Christ lives in me."

A warrior who has died to self is formidable.

Now, about that preparation and planning . . .

In Ephesians 6, Paul wrote about being ready for battle and specifically about putting on spiritual armor. What is this "armor" that we are to put on, that we are to clothe ourselves with before we engage with life? It's all pretty basic, really, but putting it on doesn't happen by itself and God won't do it for us—we are called to do something, to be proactive.

We're told to stand firm, having put on:

1. The Belt of Truth

There are no lack of false voices and false messages from the world, our flesh, and the devil to fill our minds, so we're going to have to be proactive to prevent them from informing how we think. Where do we go for truth? In John 17:17, Jesus said to the Father, "Your word is truth." The truth is the Word of God, the Bible. We have to read it to know it . . . to put it on.

"Putting on the truth" is taking it into our minds, reflecting on it, and standing behind it. No SEAL got prepared for his mission in one sitting. It takes months of study and preparation. The same is true of the believer and the spiritual warfare that will comprise all the days of the average Christian life.

Your mission is to open the Bible every day and read from it. And don't read it for intellectual fulfillment, or to be a better debater, or to impress others with the extent of your Bible knowledge. Approach the Bible with a single question in mind: *Dear God, what are you trying to teach me about how to live my life today?*

Remember, absorbing truth is a lifelong pursuit. Receive

truth at the pace God wants to impart it to you. Don't demand that God fill you at your pace. But to be filled with truth, you have to show up for training. Read the Word every day!

2. The Breastplate of Righteousness

Want your vital organs protected in hand-to-hand combat? Better put on your breastplate. Our righteousness comes from one place: Jesus Christ. The only success we can have against the enemy of our souls is after we've put on the breastplate of righteousness—after we've come to Jesus and received his righteousness in exchange for our rags. We know our breastplate has been well placed when we rely on the righteousness of Jesus for our standing rather than our own righteousness.

At some point, the Enemy is going to try to cause you to become discouraged and to believe that you don't measure up—that you're a failure that God will never accept. Which is all true if we're talking about God evaluating you on your own merits. Before the Almighty, our righteousness is foul—filthy rags, the Bible (Isa. 64:6) calls it (you should look up that reference in the Hebrew to see just how foul it really is!).

But our breastplate isn't constructed from the substance of our own righteousness. It is crafted from the righteousness of Jesus Christ. That is a breastplate that can sustain the heavy blows. We need to "put it on," which is to hear the gospel, believe it, and receive Jesus' righteousness for our rags; and then we need to keep that truth at the forefront of our mind every time the Enemy tries to stab us with a destructive lie. When God sees us, he is now actually viewing his own righteousness.

3. Gospel of Peace

This is the message and purpose of the spiritual warrior. It's why he's fighting a battle in the first place. He didn't choose the fight but he's in it, nevertheless, and he needs to remember why he's fighting and what he hopes to accomplish—living out and spreading the gospel of peace.

What is the gospel of peace? It's the way anyone can find peace with God, receiving the payment for the penalty of their sin by faith—what Jesus did on the cross. I like what Mark Twain once said: "It ain't those parts of the Bible I can't understand that bother me, it is the parts that I do understand." Jesus said, "I am the way and the truth and the Life. No one comes to the Father except through me" (John 14:6). This is the message of the spiritual warrior—he is communicating all the way to peace with God.

4. Shield of Faith

When the night of battle closes in, the shield of faith (the confidence in what God has said) is vital for protection. Spears of doubt will come from out of nowhere. Faith is what will see us through. Does God love us when tragedy strikes? Satan says, "No!" God's Word says, "Yes!"

The shield of faith (settled belief in what God has said) will prevent you from being a victim of the Enemy's spear. Faith equals belief. We effectively use the shield of faith when we refuse to be persuaded by circumstances, doubts, and arguments that contradict the Bible, the Word of God.

5. Helmet of Salvation

We're going to take some knocks on the head. Without salvation, we'll never stand. It's a vital piece of defensive armor but needs to be accompanied by the rest. First Thessalonians 5:8 speaks of the helmet as the hope of salvation. Yes, the battle is hard at times, but we maintain hope that sees us through the darkest moonless night. We know where we're going.

The helmet of salvation is our hope in God's promises—that he'll do what he said he will do. We have a hope and a future. He has prepared a place for us in heaven, and he promises to be with us every step of the way here on earth.

6. The Sword of the Spirit (which is the Word of God)

How are you with your sword? Clumsy? Careless? Unfamiliar? Skilled? Accurate? The Bible is the sword of the Spirit. Practice (reading/studying/obeying) makes perfect—and you play (fight/war) how you practice. Why would God instruct us to put on armor unless he understood that we are headed for an impending battle? Will we yield to his directive or maintain our own sense of control, like that crazy soldier on the battlefield, acting like we're on vacation? Here are a few suggestions to help you get better with your sword:

- *Regular Bible reading.* Putting even a little of God's Word in your heart and mind each day can have a radical effect on how you experience the daily events of your life. It provides perspective that cannot be found in any other source.

- *Memorization*. King David said, "I have hidden your word in my heart that I might not sin against you" (Ps. 119:11). Pick a verse per day/week and commit it to memory. I suggest Psalm 1 as a great set of verses to start with.
- *Meditation on the Word of God*. Pick a short passage and ask the Holy Spirit to reveal to you a deeper understanding.

How many times have you found yourself struggling with life's circumstances, your own failures, unfaithful friends, persecution for what you believe—bewildered at where life has taken you? Being confused, frustrated, or filled with anger at what we're forced to deal with is a natural, human response. These circumstances and experiences violate our sense of personal sovereignty and control.

God encourages us to see our struggles with a more mature perspective—an eternal perspective. He has tried to get us to understand there is far more going on than what we see in the physical realm. The only reason our circumstances catch us off guard (said another way, the only reason we are defeated or react sinfully to them) is because we don't bother to listen to what God has said about them before they happen.

We tend to like our understanding of the world better than what God tells us about it. Our thinking is confined to the present, physical moment and to the specific circumstance, but God has not been unclear on the source of our struggles.

So which life circumstances and relationships fit into the

spiritual realm? All of them! Our true nature is spiritual and our existence, eternal. As a Christian, a follower of Jesus Christ, you live in a state of spiritual war—it is what your life actually is. We now know which particular enemies we are specifically warned against: the world, the flesh, and the devil. And we've been told what to do: arm ourselves.

———

SIXTH STEP TO A SURRENDERED LIFE: Define your mission and wear your armor.

Action Step

Take some time to think about what your day looks like if you view it as a battle, a series of events that will move you either further from or closer to God. Then think about each piece of armor that you just read about and how it would help you win these individual battles.

Prayer

Father, I have had many difficult days in my life. But the days where the difficulty could be traced to my decisions all had one thing in common: I did not put on my armor. Please help me to not only die each day to my desires but also to start each day preparing myself for the battle that is sure to come. You have given me everything I need to fight and you have even designed the battle to move me closer to you. But I ruin everything when I am not prepared as you would have me prepare. You have given me truth, righteousness, peace, faith, salvation, and your written Word. Help me respect and prepare for battle like a SEAL does for his mission. And let me consider success the fulfillment of your mission.

SEALs don't train alone. There's a reason for that and it's no different for the Christian going into this spiritual battle/struggle we call everyday life. The most effective training you can do is as a part of a community. That's how God designed it. He intended for you and me to live in fellowship, not only with him, but with each other. Unfortunately, the wrong community can lead to the least effective training or no training at all.

There are no "Lone Rangers" in the body of Christ. Struggle is a team sport. You need to be a team player. How does that look?

Seven

Struggle Is a Team Sport

THERE WAS NO WAY THE BASKETBALL GAME was going to be boring tonight. All week people were talking about "him," the new ace forward from the other team. The hard wooden seats of the bleachers were filling up, and we quickly found a spot not too far from the floor where my friend's son's team was getting ready for the game.

I started scanning the other team as they warmed up. It was easy to see who everyone was talking about. He was a real standout, but as I watched him, I'll admit, a slight grin broke out across my face. It didn't take long before I knew we were going to win the basketball game. Even in the warm-up phase, it was easy to see that this kid, good as he was, was the genuine article—a certified ball hog!

In a game designed to be won by coordination and working together, maximizing each other's strengths, this kid was determined to play solo; and as I predicted, by the end of the first half, it was clear that his team would not win the game.

When it comes to struggling, when it comes to life, are you a ball hog? Are you the one who is determined to go it alone? Like I said in the beginning, I don't like sharing my struggles, messes, and failures. Who does? But if we are going to learn to walk God's way—through our struggles—we have to be willing to do it God's way. And when it comes to the trials that life throws at us, or that we bring on ourselves . . .

Struggle is a team sport.

Most of us have had experiences in church that take all the fun out of playing on the same team. Who hasn't felt the sharp knife of betrayal, of having been too open too early, only to discover later that the person you confided in didn't have your back? *Experience can make us wise, but too often it makes us hard.*

My friend Marsha struggled as a new wife and mother with several tasks relating to managing her home. As a young woman, she felt embarrassed that tasks, which came so easily and naturally to others, were overwhelming to her. She was raised in a loving home—too loving, as it turned out. With so much done for her by her own mother, she was ill equipped to manage her own home. Thankfully, a couple of older women from the church came to her and offered to help her—to show her how she could become more organized and productive. Admittedly, it was a little embarrassing revealing her secret failures to these women at first, but Marsha humbled herself and was ready to grow.

It was a great plan. Marsha was so encouraged . . . until she happened onto a conversation . . . behind the slightly ajar door, where the two women laughed and joked about her incompetence.

The net effect of hits like that makes us impervious to real relationships. Facing the pain of false relationships does that. It's just not worth the cost. Billy Joel was wrong about a lot of things, but he was right about honesty in relationships: honesty is such a lonely word. To this day, Marsha will tell you she trusts no one. It's sad and God does want her to grow in this area, but at one level, I can't blame her.

Let me emphasize again that this is a messy process. It is not safe and contained. All people struggle, so you will be surrounded by even more problems. As much as the idea of community was never more positive than in the months following the car accident with my son, I must also say that I have never received more criticism and judgment from the Christian community than during this same time period.

When you let your struggles be known, you will also be inundated by the "answer people." These are the people who can solve all your problems without even knowing you. They are followed closely by the Bible-verse people who simplify your entire life into one or two verses, which, though true, are more likely to incite violence toward them than peace within you. These people are closely related to the "I" club who will instantly relate your story to something in their own lives and then proceed to talk about themselves until you are nauseated. And even the people who act as your friends will occasionally hurt you.

I've lived it, and I'm sure you have too. If we're not careful, we become like a sea anemone, recognizing the slightest touch as a dangerous threat and pulling into ourselves.

So, are we going to go with our experience and pull in like

that sea anemone? At least we'll be safe, right? No, not really . . . if we're honest with ourselves. Even though it might feel safe in the moment, closing ourselves off from true relationship is a place of profound powerlessness. Illusions often provide momentary comfort. The fact is, a sea anemone can't find nourishment pulling into itself and staying there, and neither can you.

The results are always the same when in our hearts we retreat to some desert island. You begin to starve, then you give up, then you die. Not an option for the believer, but neither is avoiding struggles. They're either coming or already here. We were designed to love and to be loved. So what do we do?

The life of surrender isn't a life based on achieving equilibrium in our feelings. It's not a path to wholeness based on how I perceive reality and decide how to proceed. If we are to be truly surrendered, as believers, it must be to what we are told to do. Not what I say or think, or how I feel when struggles come, but what I am instructed to do. Where do we get that kind of information?

It's not complicated: the Bible.

We will only find strength to struggle well if we surrender our will, our determination to walk in isolation and do what we think best, and embrace the instruction found in the Scriptures—the sword of the Spirit. What do they have to say about this?

- Confess your sins to each other and pray for each other. (James 5:16)

- Carry each other's burdens, and in this way you will fulfill the law of Christ. (Gal. 6:2)

Are you feeling the heavy weight of a struggle or burden right now? God never intended for you to carry it alone. In fact, he doesn't want you to. Certainly, it can feel like it sometimes. But God wants us to walk together—to keep risking it—to experience the lightness of sharing our failures, struggles, wounds, and burdens, and in so doing, receive a blessing and be a blessing to others.

You risked it before . . . Is God asking you to risk it again?

Certainly, we need to be wise, not being careless with whom we are willing to divulge sensitive information. But when it comes to our struggles, God wants to help us, and his plan often comes in a disguise that we typically recognize as risk—a person. If God's answer to sharing your burden and helping you through your struggles (namely, a person he brought into your life) is going to be able to provide the help God intended, the voices of fear and pride have to be silenced and the voice of truth has to be listened to. If we are to bear one another's burdens, we need to be willing to confess our faults, shortcomings, failures, fears, and wounds to each other.

Where can I find people like that . . . people I can trust . . . people who will have my back after they know my whole story? Where are they?

I've got to be honest with you. I don't know . . .

. . . but God does. He knows right where they are, at this very instant, and he wants you to walk in fellowship with them.

———

Carol loved the beauty found on her favorite walk along the seawall at Stanley Park near her home in Vancouver, British Columbia. But all that beauty wasn't designed to fill that place of growing emptiness in her heart. She had moved to Vancouver a few months back, having landed a job cleaning eighty-year-old Mrs. Guggenheimer's expansive house. Day after day, Carol went to work, made serious money, and by degrees became seriously lonely. Carol became desperate to find Christian community, Christian fellowship. And trying out church after church each Sunday wasn't helping.

Carol was bumping up against a fact many people come to realize only after being disillusioned: real Christian fellowship—the kind described in the New Testament—is as rare as healthy foods can be at church potlucks. But it had to be out there, didn't it? Didn't the Bible say to "love one another fervently" (1 Peter 1:22 NKJV)? How was she going to find fellowship like that?

One day, after about the sixth Sunday of searching, Carol went back to her apartment and cried herself to sleep, pleading with God, "Please, oh God, my Father, bring me someone who will care about me, who will love me, who I can love, who I can share with, walk with, grow with, please."

Dutifully rising the next morning, Carol went to work at Mrs. Guggenheimer's. *How oddly quiet the house is this morning*, she thought when she arrived. Then, pushing her cleaning supplies through the door to the morning room, she immediately started, "Oh, I'm so sorry for interrupting you."

Mrs. Guggenheimer looked up sweetly, saying, "Please

don't be sorry. You're not interrupting me. I was just doing a little reading here in the gospel of John. Do you have a Bible?"

Mrs. Guggenheimer is a Christian? Suddenly, Carol realized that God's provision for her was right before her eyes, and for the next year, Mrs. G and Carol met every day for fellowship in the Word and in Christ.

We never know how God will answer our prayers to find community. Sometimes, perhaps more often than not, it comes from the most unexpected places.

Ask and ye shall receive.

I hate to say this, but for many people, finding real community will never happen on Sunday morning. You'll find great music, powerhouse preaching, entertaining stories, big programs often reaching past the local community to the world—orphanages in Africa, building projects in Mexico, food distribution in Bangladesh—but Christian community and fellowship across the aisle on Sunday morning? Not going to happen.

Fellowship won't happen until you and I spend time with each other. Watching a show designed to delight the spectators on Sunday morning doesn't qualify.

I'm not saying it's an incontrovertible fact, but taken as a whole, you can't find true community in a large church unless you become involved with smaller groups of people within the church. We need relationships, not acquaintances. Real community starts with knowing people and being known. Of course, this gets right back to "I'd rather have a root canal . . ."

We have to be willing to defeat the impulse to hide from each other. We have to recognize the impulse to live a hidden life as one that does not come from heaven, but from the other place. Because until you and I are ready to be known, until you and I are prepared to defeat the fear of someone knowing who we are, we will never be ready—we'll never be able to enter into true community, wherever we may find it.

God knows what you need. He also knows who you need. On the front end of this journey of surrender and freedom, many of us won't have anyone we can immediately turn to. But when it comes to what and who we need, God is not absent and uninterested. He is ever present for you, just like he was for Carol.

"I will never leave you nor forsake you," God said in Joshua 1:5. If we feel as though God has left us, however, maybe it's time to consider that we've moved away from him instead of the other way around. Had Carol stopped her search for true Christian community and fellowship after the disappointments she experienced, she might have concluded that God had given up on her, that he didn't care anymore and wasn't listening to her prayers. How wrong she would have been.

How we may be feeling about our present circumstances can never be the basis on which we evaluate God's love for us.

Consider the sparrow, a bird of relatively little value in New Testament times. Jesus says not a single sparrow falls to the ground apart from the Father's notice. Remember, he says,

You are of far more value than a sparrow.

He knows your circumstances. He knows our need. He cares about those wounds that just won't heal, that impossible relationship that continues to stab, that struggle that looms ahead larger than a mountain. In seeking the path of shared burdens, go to the Father and ask him for help—ask him to bring into your life that person or people who will come alongside you and be both a comfort and the strength in your life you need.

God knows where they are. He knows who they are. He wants his people to share burdens. Ask him to reveal those people to you, right now. And be like Carol. Don't stop until he reveals them to you.

No, it's not comfortable. Maturity never comes without cost. *So*, you may be wondering now, *why do I have to involve others? Why do I have to risk another effort at relationship? Because the last time I attempted to do so taught me the value of stuffing my troubles.*

When Jesus was asked, "Which is the greatest commandment?" he answered that we are to "love the Lord your God with all your heart," a phrase that encapsulates the first four commandments. Jesus quickly followed it up with what he called the second greatest commandment—"love your neighbor as yourself"—which sums up the remaining six commandments (Matt. 22:36–39). According to Jesus, the most important two things we must do are to love God and love our neighbor. We were made to love, but what happens when we don't? What happens when the power of self-focus, temptations of the enemy, and the world are given access to our hearts?

When we don't love we open ourselves up to the cares and influences of the world, replacing our desire to be in loving relationship with God and others with cheap counterfeits like achievement, money, sex, recognition, and the pursuit of happiness, however elusive it is.

When we don't walk how and with whom we were intended to walk, our lives become full of pursuits that can never satisfy. We intensify our pursuit and find ourselves given to idols that only draw us away further. We'll ensure the picture appears intact, maintaining surface relationships, but emptiness and loneliness eventually erode every effort.

So, after failed attempts, false starts, and frustration, why should we try again to pursue Christian community and fellowship?

We do it, first of all, because God has said this is how he wants it done. God's way is always best—even after we screw it up. If we won't share, we can't bear (one another's burdens). He doesn't want his followers living lives of disconnected independence, regardless of how lonely the average person is in the happening megachurch, or in the small Bible church down the street, for that matter. We were made for each other—made to love—to walk in fellowship, love, and unity.

In the countless circumstances and trials that encompassed my family's journey after a horrific car accident, God was right there, loving us through the love of people in the church. Whether we needed our roof replaced after a storm blew a tree on it, a van for transporting our quadriplegic son, or just someone to pray with, God repeatedly showed his love to us through other people. Whatever our needs, God meets them through Christian community.

But there are other reasons. We are to risk it (with those we believe God would have us to be open) because God isn't at work only in my life or only in your life. God desires to work his will in the life of the other person as well. When we open up and share our need, our emptiness, our loneliness, our financial need, our pain—risking relationship—we create a safe place for someone else to share what fear had prevented him from being open about.

Carol eventually got around to asking God for help after her exhausting efforts visiting church after church. We can start with prayer right now! Again, God knows what and who we need, so let's ask him.

When you do seek a local church for true Christian fellowship, look for a group of believers who place a premium on open, honest fellowship through relationships in the church rather than programs and activities, even if they sound fantastic. Don't confuse activities with fellowship. It's easy to find a church where you can find something to do. The local church must be a place where we actively practice our beliefs, not just show up and be entertained. The apostle Peter said it like this: "Love one another fervently with a pure heart" (1 Peter 1:22 NKJV).

That word *fervently* comes from the word *furnace*—the furnace used in refining gold. It's an intense, refining fire that burns away impurities, leaving only pure gold. You and I were made to be refined in the crucible of fervent, loving relationships.

It's important to be part of a church that is dedicated to biblical teaching, but there's a danger here too. No doubt you've been to a church so committed to doctrinal purity that they are clear as ice and colder than frozen steel, or the other extreme—so warm and fuzzy with feel-good teaching you couldn't find a conviction there if it came up and bit you. A healthy church places a higher priority on love than agreement on every doctrinal point—just like it teaches in 1 Corinthians 13. But don't let yourself fall prey to the spirit of the age that says doctrine isn't important.

When you find all these things in a church, you have to hang in there! Real relationships are a lot like a garden. They take time.

Have you ever picked a fresh, deep-red cherry tomato right off the vine? Bite into one and the flavor is so intense it shoots right to the back of your mouth—out of this world! But that tomato didn't just show up. It started as a seedling four months before and was nurtured every step of the way. There's nothing quick or particularly rewarding about preparing the soil in the spring. It's a lot of hard work.

My friend Bill has a garden that reminds me of Eden. I walk into it and am amazed. Ask Bill how he does it and he'll point to a bucket in the middle of the garden where it all starts. Now, I don't mean to be gross, but Bill has a cow (bucket, cow . . . I'll let your imagination fill in the rest). As I said, relationships are a lot like a garden. Weeds grow quickly and without much effort. For something beautiful to grow, time is necessary. Give those relationships time. And just like Carol found, be prepared to discover that they can appear in the most unexpected places.

How do you want to be treated? With grace, I'll bet. I love

how a friend put it: Always expect the best but accept less. People don't walk on water or turn water into wine. Let's leave the expectation of perfection with Jesus and pray that others will do the same with you. Let's not be hard on the people Jesus is asking us to walk with. If we're demanding a standard that we ourselves couldn't possibly live up to, all we'll achieve is driving people away.

This is easy to do if we remember one last thing that is hard to keep in mind: you're always interacting with Jesus. Sometimes he shows up as the sweet lady with Alzheimer's. Sometimes he shows up as the felon to whom God gave a second chance. Sometimes he shows up as that bratty kid who bugs the soup out of you. But no matter who you are interacting with, from God's perspective, he is Jesus. And when we're interacting with the one who was tortured and died for you and me, it's easy to love and to extend grace.

How does this idea of interacting in community fit directly with surrender? Or even with dying? These notions are tied together with two principles that are key for succeeding in both personal surrender to God and in integrating our mess into the larger community mess. That's right. Mess upon mess. If you view these processes any other way, you will never be able to move forward with any level of authenticity.

Pride must die. The first principle that is key to succeeding in both private and public surrender is the death of pride. Just as trying to look good for God is a waste of time, so, too, is pretending you have it all together for other people. When I first met my agent, I was in the process of writing a book about my family in an effort to show the goodness of God and other people. We were excited to work on this project together.

But very early in our relationship I felt the need to share with him some personal problems that I thought he should be aware of. I shared with him some struggles in my marriage. I talked with him about a few other issues, which I felt he should know if we were going to be partners in this work. He did not just nod his head and say, "That's okay." Nor did he shake his head in disgust. He asked some very pointed questions. I answered them as honestly as I could. And then we prayed together. This would be the first of many prayers that we would pray in person and mostly over the phone. He has always listened to me, challenged me to be godly, and prayed with and for me. I have always tried to do the same for him.

In the past three or four years we have been through more tough issues together than I would even care to think about. We do not always agree. But I always trust him. I value my relationship with him a great deal. But there is no way that our relationship would have been nearly as fruitful if I had not shared my "dirty little secrets" in the very beginning. It is important that we learn to share, but it is equally important that we handle what is told to us by others with the strength and grace that my agent has always done with me.

Always remember that community and relationship work both ways. The second death that is common to both private and public surrender is the voluntary death of independence. Have you ever actually tried to "pull yourself up by your bootstraps"? Is it possible? Even if it is, it is not ideal. Why not just extend a hand and allow someone to help you up? It is a myth that we succeed on our own. There is no such thing as a self-made man.

I recently watched some of the NFL Hall of Fame induction speeches. If anyone could outwardly appear as if they are capable of doing things on their own, it would be professional football players. And yet the list of people that these "self-made men" thank lasts so long they must have their time limited by the event organizers. Being in community is to let go of your independence, but it also means you are not merely dependent either. We should all try to be mentoring someone and be mentored by someone. The independent spirit must die and give way to one that is interdependent. As we die to ourselves and let Christ live through us, we then pass this spirit on to others.

It's easy for us to think of the life of surrender to God as some big, flashy spiritual pursuit. The longer I live, the more I'm convinced that God is less interested in the big gestures, the gargantuan feats of spiritual endurance, or throwing myself at spiritual problems halfway around the world. The life of surrender to God—the life of spiritual purpose and meaning—is surrendering to his will, his way, doing what he said about loving my neighbor. The surrendered life is the life of obedience to the clear, obvious, everyday things he asks of you and me. God is only my Lord if I obey him. He desires that you and I walk in fellowship with each other. It is his priority. It must be ours as well.

SEVENTH STEP TO A SURRENDERED LIFE: Be part of a team.

Action Step

Ask God to bring you safe people you can know and be known by, and when he does, make sure you take the initiative to connect with them. Also, find new ways to serve other people.

Prayer

God, I know you have designed me to be in community. Help me learn to not only be dependent on you but to depend on your people as well. Help me have deep, messy relationships as opposed to fake, sterile ones. Father, help me understand my need for you and my need for others. Please show me the people who need me and give me the courage to offer my help. Guide me into healthy community that is empowered by your spirit and your desires.

Eight

Surrendered . . . Really?

HOW MUCH OF US IS JESUS WILLING TO SETTLE for? This was basically the same question the rich young ruler (RYR) asked Jesus, but he didn't much like the answer he got.

When "RYR" approached Jesus and asked him, "Good teacher . . . what must I do to inherit eternal life?" (Mark 10:17), he was what most of us would consider a good young man (a good Christian in today's terms)—and he knew it. So when Jesus answered his question by saying he just had to keep the Ten Commandments, the wealthy young man confidently reported that he had done it all, from being a youth till now. But Jesus wasn't quite as impressed as the RYR was with himself.

"One thing you lack: Go your way, sell whatever you have and give to the poor, . . . take up the cross, and follow Me" (v. 21 NKJV).

Jesus said it would cost everything, down to the last penny, and after that was spent, his life was next . . . Remember that cross? The answer is the same today. *Jesus will never settle for a piece of you.* And he doesn't need our money. He requires everything. Complete surrender.

Most of us would rather keep the money. It's fun to be rich and young.

After the water-to-wine miracle at the wedding in Cana, the Passover was soon to take place and Jesus made his way down to Jerusalem. Coming into the temple, he couldn't avoid seeing the market stalls where various animals were being sold to worshipers as well as the money changers enjoying the great business environment created by the feast. The travelers from all over the Roman Empire needed to exchange their foreign currency into the local coin and purchase animals for sacrifice.

Jesus looked around, disgusted at it all—livestock milling around, people bartering for better deals on a pair of doves, someone else loudly protesting the exorbitant fees for changing money . . . and the smell of livestock . . . barnyard excrement everywhere.

He came to worship God but couldn't because of all the noise, all the distraction, all the degradation . . . all the sin.

When it comes to the temple, how clean is clean enough for Jesus?

As quietly as he came, Jesus left, but his mind was not at rest. In his chest a seething anger burned in righteous indignation. He was compelled to do something—to act—to work with his hands. Before long, some quality cord was being tested for strength by those strong, calloused carpenter hands. If you are going to braid a whip, better use good-quality cord. Soon, the weapon was ready. Can you imagine Jesus cracking the whip a time or two, testing it out to get the feel of it before reentering the temple compound? I can.

The first time he entered peacefully. His second coming was something different. We're going to have to leave our "Sweet Little Gentle Jesus" illusion at the door. He came in a fury of righteous rage, brandishing that whip, driving out all who bought and sold, all of the livestock, and throwing over the tables of the money changers.

"Don't make my father's house a house of merchandise!" Perhaps you believe he said this quietly and demurely, hoping he wouldn't offend anyone. Are you kidding me?! He yelled those words! There wasn't anyone present (admittedly inferred from the passage) who didn't immediately experience the fury of the enraged Son. The party was over, and the mayhem ensued in an effort to avoid the sting of the whip Jesus made and used.

The disciples watched (wide-eyed, I'm guessing), because as they observed their teacher raging, the scene brought to mind something they had read in the Scriptures:

"Zeal for Your house has eaten me up" (Ps. 69:9 NKJV).

Have you ever been so focused on something that it feels like it is literally eating out your insides? Decorum is out the window. Jesus was so totally consumed by his zeal for his Father's dwelling place that he had to—was compelled to—throw out every person, drive out every animal, knock over every money changer's table, and clean out every corner of the temple where these unholy activities were taking place. Nothing was safe from his righteous fury, and he didn't stop until everyone engaged in these things was running for the exits.

The temple—the Father's dwelling place—was that sacred, that set apart, that holy. The cleanliness of the Father's dwelling place, his temple, was so critical that Jesus would not stop until every inch of it was cleansed from this defilement.

Jesus isn't interested in a mostly cleansed temple with only 49 percent devoted to money changing and a few birds and sheep defecating in the corner. He is not that concerned with democracy. When it comes to the temple's use and purpose, a tithe of a portion of the temple isn't acceptable. Jesus wants it all—every square inch. That's what he made the whip for, what he came to do, and he didn't stop until the job was done.

"Go, Jesus! Take 'em down."

We know he's eventually going to be crucified, but it's kind of fun to see him doing the big smack down on his enemies. Would I have been on Jesus' side? Oh yeah, definitely. It's only natural to imagine being on the winning side, but let's ask ourselves: How do we actually live?

Not too many years later in AD 70, the Romans completely destroyed the temple. They carried away all its immense treasures and leveled the building to the ground. Little did they know they were fulfilling a prophecy of Jesus' from Luke 21:6: "As for what you see here, the time will come when not one stone will be left on another; every one of them will be thrown down." And so it was. The Romans didn't leave a single stone standing on the foundations of the temple. Following this destruction, the Jews were dispersed over the world and the temple has never been rebuilt.

So keeping the temple clean isn't an issue anymore, right? Wrong.

Jesus is as concerned today about the cleanliness of the temple as he was while on earth. And he's just as demanding as he always was. A tithe of some percentage of the temple won't do. He wants it all—every corner, every crevice. No amount of filth, however minuscule, is acceptable to him. The geography and location may have changed, but Jesus' perspective hasn't, even though the physical temple is gone. But there is another . . .

> Or do you not know that your body is a temple of the Holy Spirit who is in you, whom you have from God, and that you are not your own? (1 Cor. 6:19 NASB)

The message is clear. My physical body is inhabited by the Spirit of God—literally. He lives in me . . . and in you. It's a wild truth.

So where do we get the idea that a little sin in God's dwelling place is okay? Isn't this how we often live? Telling ourselves that, for the most part, we belong to God? There wasn't one money changer or seller of livestock in the temple courtyard that would have said anything different.

By all means, the temple belongs to Jehovah—it's his dwelling place.

We often get the words right, but words won't cut it when Jesus is looking on the inside.

But then again, why wouldn't we be comfortable with a little sin when preachers everywhere tickle our ears by telling us that a little barnyard excrement in our lives is no big deal because, you know, we're under grace?

Since when (and where) did the Bible teach that being

under grace means that the sin in our lives is no big deal? We need to remember that Jesus doesn't mess around. He came to clean house. He wouldn't settle for having most of the rich young ruler, and he won't settle for having most of us.

It's all or nothing with Jesus.

Are You Surrendered to Something or to Someone?

He was impossible to miss, leaning up against the wall near the entrance to the mall, the smell being first to introduce the presence of this collection of bad choices. The truth can't be helped. He stank. Long, greasy curls reached down to stooped shoulders in dull black clumps, speckled with premature gray. A soiled gray hoodie, the victim of too many spin cycles, clung desperately to nervous bones held together by little more than sinew and skin.

Cloudy eyes that knew too much, cunning as rats, glowered through the protective barrier of dreadlocks, constantly assessing the vulnerability of passersby, careful not to waste a forlorn glance on the businessman with the hardened edge, the shopper fresh from the salon with a cool air, or the mother distracted with three young kids. No, he was working. He had to be efficient. Time was running out, desperation growing with every passing minute.

Sitting near the entrance after dropping $4.50 for my sixteen-ounce white chocolate mocha, I had no intention of giving him money—of giving him anything. But I still wanted to watch. I knew his game—just another junkie after the next fix. What was it—crack, heroin, meth? Didn't really matter. They're all the same, and there's nothing you can do if some- one is determined to yield his life to addiction.

But for some reason, today was different from other times. Who hasn't seen an addict, spent of life and purpose, in desper- ate pursuit of that which is completely consuming his life? Yet I couldn't take my eyes off of him, wondering what his life might have been. We had to be about the same age. What could have been so captivating to completely engulf his life in this one pur- suit? What a waste.

Let's face it, there's nothing quite as disgusting as a junkie near the end of his run. He'd probably sell his grandmother to shoot up one more time.

But suddenly I felt guilty. I'm a Christian—aren't I supposed to be compassionate for people like that? And for a moment, compassion did fill my thoughts. Where would I be without God's grace? Where would he be with it? The fact is, we're all variations on the same theme.

But then something strange happened, something un- expected, something disorienting. Have you ever been in a pitch-black room when someone instantly turns on the bright- est lights? With everything illuminated, you can see nothing. But then, gradually the room and its furnishings come into focus. It was like that, staring at the junkie.

Could I have been hearing correctly?

All along, I was pretty sure the junkie needed me, or at least he could benefit from knowing me. I had a lot to teach him, a lot to offer. I certainly didn't want or need any part of him. Sometimes it's a gentle wind that blows over our house of cards, sometimes it's a tornado.

Am I hearing correctly? Really, God . . . really? That junkie has something to teach me? He's addicted and out of control. What could I possibly learn from him?

God's response shook me to my core. *That junkie is surrendered to his god. Do you pursue me with the same devotion that he pursues his god?*

When it comes to God's way, you can just about always count on it being exactly the opposite of what naturally comes to mind. An addict is a pretty negative image, generally speaking, but on closer consideration, we might come to understand something about our lack of commitment and the standard to which we've been called.

Think about it. What is a junkie, really, but someone pursuing his god with reckless, purposeful abandon? An addict is completely sold out and surrendered. This guy had given up everything just to have one more encounter with, one more taste of, his god. Nothing will distract him from his pursuit. He didn't have the slightest concern for anything else—it was focus on his god, 24/7. A genuine addict doesn't care one bit for his life; he only cares for his god.

"Anyone who loves their father or mother more than me is not worthy of me; anyone who loves their son or daughter more than me is not worthy of me. . . . Whosoever finds their life will lose it, and whoever loses their life for my sake will find it" (Matt. 10:37, 39).

Kind of sounds like that addict, doesn't it?

An addict is surrendered to the service of one entity. A junkie can't live without being infused with his god. Without taking it into his body, either orally or through some other method, the junkie can't function.

In John 6, Jesus told a crowd, "Very truly I tell you, unless you eat the flesh of the Son of Man and drink his blood, you have no life in you. Whoever eats my flesh and drinks my blood has eternal life. . . . For my flesh is real food and my blood is real drink. Whoever eats my flesh and drinks my blood remains in me, and I in them" (vv. 53–56).

Imagine how all this sounded to Jesus' Jewish audience. Remember, these were strict adherents to the Mosaic law. Cannibalism? Drinking blood . . . of any kind, let alone human blood? Are you serious, Jesus?

We don't have to guess what they thought.

In verse 60, "many of his disciples said, 'This is a hard teaching. Who can accept it?'"

Sorry, Jesus, you went too far this time. (But you have to admit, it's a pretty good description for how the addict views his god. He's just got to get his god inside of his body.)

And this is what Jesus wants us to understand, wants me to understand. We've got to get him inside us . . . we've got to be willing to "eat" his flesh and "drink" his blood—to consume him and be consumed by him.

Jesus wants us to understand that until we are surrendered to him in the same way—and to the same degree that the addict is surrendered to his false god—we will miss the fulfillment and beauty of a life infused and animated by him.

No, the addict's life isn't beautiful, but that's only because the enemy of his soul managed to deceive him into thinking that the god he chose would fulfill his need. Counterfeiting is an effective line of work. And our enemy is really good at what he does. Satan always offers a counterfeit for everything God offers.

When you're sold out, all other offers pale in comparison to God or to the false god to whom you are surrendered. And this is what it is all about.

Give up. Give it all to Jesus.

> *Whoever lose their life for my sake will find it. . . . The words I have spoken to you—they are full of the spirit and life.*

—JESUS CHRIST (MATT. 10:39; JOHN 6:63)

EIGHTH STEP TO A SURRENDERED LIFE: Become addicted to your need for God.

Action Step

Think about what things in your life you "must have." Is Jesus at the top of the list? You were designed to be dependent on him and to have him alive inside of you. Call upon his Spirit within you as you go through your day.

Prayer

Lord, please help me crave your presence. Put in me a desire to be with you and depend on you at all times. Draw me back when I begin to want other things more than you. Like the addict, make it difficult for me to function when I have not taken in enough of you. Thank you for your commitment to me that is in place regardless of my commitment to you. Thank you also for heaven where I will always be in your magnificent presence.

Nine

The Battle Between the Battles

THE USS *INDIANAPOLIS* (CA-35) WAS BUILT between World War I and World War II. She was considered the pride of the navy. The boat was 610 feet long and 66 feet wide. She was built for speed and had all of the latest technology of the day. One of the reasons that the *Indianapolis* was so fast is that its displacement weight was kept to a minimum by decreasing the thickness of the armor plating on the bottom of the boat. It was a boat designed to look good and to transport dignitaries.

President Roosevelt used the *Indianapolis* as his Ship of State to transport him in his travels around South America on several occasions. She was the flagship of Admiral Wilson Brown who held the position of the head of Scouting Force whose job it was to search for and detect enemies. In 1943, the *Indianapolis* went through a major overhaul and became the flagship for

Admiral Raymond Spruance who was commander of the Fifth Fleet and the victor of the Battle of Midway. The home port of the *Indianapolis* was Pearl Harbor, though she was not there on the day of the bombing in 1941.

The USS *Indianapolis* had a long and storied history, but perhaps its most important mission occurred on July 26, 1945. It was on this date that she delivered to the island of Tinian, one of the two atomic bombs that the United States dropped on Japan to end World War II.

After successfully delivering the major components of the bomb, the ship was ordered to return to Guam where it would receive further orders. Following a brief stop in Guam, the ship was directed to rendezvous with the USS *Idaho* near the Philippines in the Leyte Gulf for a few days of gunnery practice and other training. After the training, the plan was that she was to head to Okinawa for the expected invasion of Japan. A message was sent from Guam to the USS *Idaho* to inform her of the arrival of the *Indianapolis*. This message was not able to be understood by the *Idaho* due to a poor radio connection and there was no request for clarification. Therefore, the *Idaho* never knew the *Indianapolis* was scheduled to meet it. In addition to the failed radio transmission, the *Indianapolis* also left the port in Guam unescorted by the destroyer it had requested.

The boat left the base on a course of 262 degrees and was cruising comfortably at 17 knots. Captain Charles McVay was implementing the standard zigzag pattern that was a common form of defense against enemy vessels but decided to abandon this maneuver as there were no apparent threats on this voyage.

At 12:14 a.m. on July 30, near the halfway point between Guam and the Leyte Gulf, the *Indianapolis* was struck by two of the six torpedoes fired by an I-58 Japanese submarine.

The first torpedo blew up the bow of the ship. The second torpedo hit the middle of the ship near a powder magazine and a fuel tank. This led to an explosion that knocked out all electrical power on the ship, including all ability to send a signal for help (though a radioman would later say that several SOS messages were sent before the power went out). The ship sunk in approximately twelve minutes.

Of the 1,197 officers and men on board, it is estimated that approximately 300 men died on board the ship while just under 900 men made it to the sea alive that morning. It would be four brutal and terrifying days before help arrived. A series of errors led to a lack of recognition that the *Indianapolis* had not arrived at its intended destination, and the men were, in fact, accidentally discovered and heroically rescued by military men who happened to be in the area at that time. Another 600 men died in the water due to injuries from the explosion, starvation, dehydration, and drowning. It is believed that several hundred of the men were eaten by sharks as they floated helplessly in the sea. Of the 900 men who went into the sea following the early morning attack, only 317 remained alive long enough to be rescued.

The whole incident went unreported for two weeks and was finally made public on August 15, 1945. Not coincidentally, this was also the date that President Truman announced the Japanese surrender. While the whole incident remains a controversial part of US military history, one thing we know for sure is that a ship built for war was not behaving like it was at war and the consequences were monumental.

The captain of the *Indianapolis* was ultimately blamed for the tragedy, though there was plenty of blame to go around. He was not told that the USS *Underhill* had been torpedoed in the same area just prior to his ship leaving Guam. Not only was he denied the traditional destroyer escort that he requested, but his ship had no antisubmarine detection equipment. Captain Charles McVay would suffer a court-martial and became the final victim of the sinking of the *Indianapolis* when he committed suicide much later in his life.

Somehow, in between the successful mission to deliver an atomic bomb on July 26 and the end of World War II just over a month later, the US Navy suffered the largest single disaster at sea in its entire history.

Why are we looking at this story? The main reason is that it reminds us that things do not always go as planned. This is obviously true when our intended mission is a failure. But it is also true that there can still be some major pitfalls even when our mission is successful. There are daily battles going on that often stay beneath our radar. They may not be the ones we share with others, but they often have the same consequences as the battles that tend to dominate our thinking. As we learn to die to ourselves and live for God and for others, we put ourselves in line with principles that will lead to a lifestyle consistent with the teachings of the Bible. But this is only the beginning of the battles to follow.

More Than What You Expect

I was a psychotherapist for many years, and with each patient I went through a similar process. I did a lot of listening, followed by a little bit of analyzing, and then the two of us would put together a plan of action. When we reached agreement on the plan, you could see the peace that came with both newfound clarity and an action plan being applied to a previously painful and confusing situation.

And then came the question that seemed to surprise almost everyone.

"Could you please tell me how you are going to mess this up?"

My clients usually initially viewed this as a lack of confidence in their ability to be successful. This was not the case at all. I had simply learned that virtually nothing in life goes as planned. There are always hiccups. We also tend to make the same kinds of mistakes. What I was trying to do was to get the person to look at some of the things that could go wrong and then we would make a plan to attack these circumstances as well.

One time I was working with a girl who had to confront a roommate about not paying rent. She was afraid of the other girl's reaction and continually avoided the conversation. We made a plan for the conversation and picked a day and time. But we were not done. We then discussed some worst-case scenarios and made a plan for how to respond to each of them. This way we were ready for something to go wrong and even had ideas about what some of those things could be.

When the young woman came back for her next appointment, I could not wait to ask her how things went. She started to laugh and I smiled as I anticipated her success story. She went on to tell me that she had the conversation at the date and time we planned and that she said exactly what we talked about.

"What happened?" I asked.

She laughed again and said, "She punched me in the face."

"Why is this funny?"

"I was so aware that things could go wrong and how I wanted to respond that when she punched me in the face it just was not that big a deal. I am pretty sure that was worse than anything we thought of, but I was still ready. And besides that, she paid me right after she hit me. Then I asked her to move out. All in all, a good day."

Not only did this woman have a plan and execute it, but she was ready for things to fall apart and was prepared. And this is where we are in this book. We need to look at what kinds of things will likely become difficult as you try to live out this surrendered life with a flesh that fights back, in a world that is inconsistent with your values, and with a devil who is still just as committed to your failure. If you think your life gets easier just because you made a one-time decision to follow Christ, you may not like the next few pages.

Common Pitfall #1

And this leads us to the first common pitfall we can learn from in the tragedy of the *Indianapolis*. Battles are always occurring whether you think you are in one or not. Even if you are not engaged in a fight, rest assured that these three enemies (world, flesh, devil) never go to sleep. And sometimes, like we see with the USS *Indianapolis*, the critical attack can occur when you think you are in between missions.

Never assume that your enemy has stopped fighting.

Or for those of you who like all of your directives in the "positive form":

Always be prepared for battle.

The men on the *Indianapolis* did not know what they were delivering to the island of Tinian. They did know their mission was to make a delivery and they successfully completed it. Their next mission involved training, and this was likely to be followed by the mission of an invasion of Japan. The error occurred when the travel between Guam and the Leyte Gulf was seemingly viewed more as downtime than wartime. This left the *Indianapolis* vulnerable to attack and ultimately hundreds of deaths. The Japanese did not view this travel route as guaranteed safe passage, and they were able to sink two ships who simply did not expect to be attacked at that time.

With this in mind, let's look at how this applies to the three main sources of our struggles, beginning with our flesh. Those desires that you have put to death will try to come back to life. The Bible talks about the ongoing conflict between the fruit of the Spirit and the fruit of the flesh:

My counsel is this: Live freely, animated and motivated by God's Spirit. Then you won't feed the compulsions of selfishness. For there is a root of sinful self-interest in us that is at odds with a free spirit, just as the free spirit is incompatible with selfishness. These two ways of life are antithetical, so that you cannot live at times one way and at times another way according to how you feel on any given day. Why don't you choose to be led by the Spirit and so escape the erratic compulsions of a law-dominated existence? (Gal. 5:16–18 MSG)

Here is what happens when we are surrendered:

But what happens when we live God's way? He brings gifts into our lives, much the same way that fruit appears in an orchard—things like affection for others, exuberance about life, serenity. We develop a willingness to stick with things, a sense of compassion in the heart, and a conviction that a basic holiness permeates things and people. We find ourselves involved in loyal commitments, not needing to force our way in life, able to marshal and direct our energies wisely. Legalism is helpless in bringing this about; it only gets in the way. Among those who belong to Christ, everything connected with getting our own way and mindlessly responding to what everyone else calls necessities is killed off for good—crucified. (vv. 22–24 MSG)

This is what happens when we are not surrendered:

It is obvious what kind of life develops out of trying to get your own way all the time: repetitive, loveless, cheap sex;

a stinking accumulation of mental and emotional garbage; frenzied and joyless grabs for happiness; trinket gods; magic-show religion; paranoid loneliness; cutthroat competition; all-consuming-yet-never-satisfied wants; a brutal temper; an impotence to love or be loved; divided homes and divided lives; small-minded and lopsided pursuits; the vicious habit of depersonalizing everyone into a rival; uncontrolled and uncontrollable addictions; ugly parodies of community. I could go on. (vv. 19–21 MSG)

A friend of mine used to say that defeating the flesh was like putting the unhealthy desire in a bag that is tied with a string. Like a snake it will continually try to slither out, and if attention is not paid to keeping the string tight, the snake will eventually escape.

The apostle Paul once asked God repeatedly to remove what he called a thorn in his flesh, but the Lord allowed it to remain (2 Cor. 12:7–9). The flesh is strong and leads to our destruction. We must put it to death every day. Failure to do so will likely lead to a surprise torpedo.

Similarly, the world is not supportive of a life surrendered to God. American culture constantly pushes self-importance, independence, personal agendas, materialism, sexual conquest, and economic identity. There is an old saying that if you are not swimming upstream you are floating downstream. A day spent going with the flow of culture is one that places us in the dangerous waters between Guam and the Leyte Gulf. The world, this side of heaven, will never stop trying to move you away from a surrendered life and trying to convince you it is all about you and the fulfillment of your desires.

Lastly, the devil will never give up until he is cast into the lake of fire. It is true that his destiny is a given. But he wants to cause as much damage to as many people as possible before his end comes to pass. He is the father of lies, and one of his most dangerous ones is to tell you all that you deserve and that following God will not provide you with these things (Gen. 3). He has great influence in this world, but he must also flee us when we command him in Jesus' name to do so. So how do we most often lose this very winnable battle? We simply choose not to fight it some days.

We must be ready every day to battle the flesh, the world we live in, and the devil. The beautiful defeat of self-will must be fought whether we think we are at battle or not. The stakes are just too high. We should no longer be surprised by the power that the flesh can seem to hold over us if we are not leading a surrendered life. Also, the more we are lulled into being comfortable with these desires, the more surprising the torpedo will be.

Common Pitfall #2

The second common pitfall to a surrendered life that we can see in the tragedy of the USS *Indianapolis* is found in its thin armor and its lack of antisubmarine radar. I am no expert in the making of seaworthy vessels, but all of the reading I did on the boat tells me that there simply was less armor than similar boats had and that the bottom of the boat was particularly vulnerable.

I think the spiritual metaphor is quite obvious here. We simply have to put on the armor of God. You may be asking why I am bringing this up again, since we already talked about it extensively in chapter 6. Let me ask you a question: How many times have you put on this armor since you read about it earlier in the book? Or did you breeze through that section thinking you already knew about it?

We need more than knowledge; we need daily application. I challenge you simply to put a piece of paper in your book at the beginning of the description of the armor of God in chapter 6. Read this section of the book on a daily basis until you are able to arm yourself every day without reading it. The shield of faith is like the radar on the USS *Indianapolis* (or not on it in this case). The shield also deflects the fiery arrows of the devil, which will help you in the daily battle with him. Here is our rule to think about:

What soldier goes to battle without armor and a weapon? Put on the armor of God every day.

We make ourselves vulnerable in ways that need not be the case. The battle is not always what you think it is, when you think it is, or where you think it is. Therefore, you must be armed and protected at all times. One last thought: If you are already dead (e.g., died to self) you cannot become a casualty of war!

Common Pitfall #3

The third common pitfall we find also involves revisiting a principle taught earlier in the book. No matter how good things are going or how bad people are treating you, you must operate in community. The messages between the *Indianapolis* and the *Idaho* were garbled and not followed up on.

The *Indianapolis* went out without the escort of a destroyer into what proved to be dangerous waters.

We are designed to function within community.

We cannot tolerate poor communication or a lack of communication with those in our community.

We tend to ask for help only when we border on being helpless, and many times we only offer help when we are asked. Ask for help and look for those in need. If you want to maintain a surrendered life on your own, your failure rate will be 100 percent. Don't just use community; be a part of one.

Just this week I have contacted several people to pray for me, and all of them prayed with me when I talked to them and pledged to do so regularly until asked to stop in the particular area. Additionally, I had to do the dreaded school fund-raiser with my daughter, and every person we asked to buy something said yes. (It helped that this year's offering was Krispy Kreme doughnuts.) I also felt led to ask someone if there was anything I could do to help him. This did not end well. He looked at me with confusion, and I think he thought I was stalking him. But at least I tried.

Community is not a part-time job. The Bible is clear that we are part of a body and that regardless of function, none of the parts can function independently of the others. Not only was the *Indianapolis* without radar and an escort, but the men were left in the water for days because no one even knew they

were missing. Pride, poor communication, and a lack of relational initiative are all enemies of healthy community and act
as a stimulus for this common pitfall of rejecting community.

Common Pitfall #4

Another unfortunate lesson that we learn from this naval
tragedy is that cover-ups and blame shifting are often present during difficult times. History showed that the captain of
the *Indianapolis* was scapegoated and purposefully kept in the
dark regarding the danger of his situation. It will be no different for you at times. You can live a surrendered life, truly seek
God's voice, and do everything you can to make every answer
to him be yes. This does not guarantee that some people will
not mistreat you, doubt your motives, lie about you, bring up
your past, reject your views, and even go out of their way just
to make sure you feel like a bad person. So what is the fourth
common pitfall of the person trying to lead a surrendered life?

Do not expect that doing right will result in you being treated
right.

My dad taught me this lesson in seventh grade. Seventh
grade was a good year. Unfortunately, I think I maxed out that
year and went downhill from there, but I digress. I got along
with pretty much everybody that year and had virtually no
peer pressure that affected me adversely. That does not mean
I was always nice, though. There was an attractive girl who
had started to get just a little bit of lightly colored hair on her
upper lip. So the other classmates and I followed the unhealthy

rule of middle school that states that all traits even slightly different must be used to try to humiliate the person possessing said trait. And so we brought a razor and a sandwich bag full of shaving cream to school and gave it to her.

The girl's humiliation did not give me the joy I was hoping for, so I apologized and tried to get the others to do so as well. They all started to say bad things about me. I was confused, so I asked my dad about the situation and he started laughing. He said, "Let me get this straight. You chose to play a practical joke with your friends. They found it funny and you did not. You told them that what they did was wrong and they treated you poorly. What did you expect, a standing ovation? Son, you cannot tell people that they are wrong and expect that very many will thank you for your insight."

Living surrendered to God is living right. Living for yourself and your lust of the moment does not work. Truly seeking God will offend a lot of people and even a lot of Christians. I talked recently with a young pastor in his twenties who was struggling with his peers (other young pastors) because he was the only one who would not go to an R-rated movie filled with violence and sexual content. They told him that his problem was that he was "too holy." Really. Show me that verse.

I know Jesus attacked the Pharisees, but that was for being religious rather than relational and surrendered to God. This pastor was just trying to avoid the old "garbage in, garbage out" issue, and he was attacked by fellow pastors. You answer to an audience of one. Stay surrendered to his commands and he will bring you new people. It is impossible to be both a pleaser of men and a follower of Christ. I know because I tried for about three decades even after my father's advice.

So what can we learn from this chapter? In a word: diligence. We have to pursue the surrendered life like a linebacker chasing down a ball carrier or my daughter trying to convince me why I will be buying her the next nail polish. It must be all out and it must be every day.

1. Always be prepared for battle.
2. Put on the armor of God every day.
3. Function in community.
4. Do not expect to be treated right for doing right.

This list is by no means exhaustive. But the story of the USS *Indianapolis* is a true one that has much to teach us about fighting an effective battle to stay surrendered to the God of Angel Armies.

NINTH STEP TO A SURRENDERED LIFE: Expect push back.

Action Step

Increase your awareness that you are always in battle and so are your opponents. The devil never takes a day off, and you cannot either. Stay vigilant in your pursuit to be surrendered to God.

Prayer

God, please help me not to be complacent in my relationship with you. Give me the eyes to see my daily battle and help me be equipped with the tools that you provide for the fight. Bring people into my life to stand beside me. Thank you that you go before me and stand behind me. Help me not to be offended but to see my mistreatment as an opportunity to demonstrate grace. Fill me with your love so that I will treat others as you would. Thank you for being with me in the battle and also for providing the time and the place where we will no longer need to battle. The gift of heaven, eternity in your presence, is worth far more than any minor disturbance that comes my way for a finite moment. I want to battle for you every day, Father. Thank you for giving me everything I need for this fight.

Ten

What Surrender Looks Like

How could he have the audacity to ask
me to give him my tomorrow?

—FROM "CRUCIFY HIM" BY SHANE & SHANE

THIS BOOK IS NOT INTENDED TO BE THEORETICAL, philosophical, or even theological. The goal is for it to be both biblical and practical. In other words, it is to be based on major truths taught in the Bible that will then inspire you to take action that will result in a radical change in your life. Mainly, that you would truly live for God and others rather than yourself. This is perhaps summed up best in Matthew 22:36–40:

> "Teacher, which is the greatest commandment in the Law?"
> Jesus replied: "'Love the Lord your God with all your heart and with all your soul and with all your mind.' This is the first and greatest commandment. And the second is like it: 'Love your neighbor as yourself.' All the Law and the Prophets hang on these two commandments."

We cannot do this on our own. We must answer the call to believe put forth in John 3:16: "For God so loved the world that he gave his one and only Son, that whoever believes in him shall not perish but have eternal life."

But as we believe in God's gift of salvation and Jesus' sacrificial death, we cannot help but become aware that we have been asked to die a similar death. Becoming a Christ-follower is not to become merely a rule follower. We must endeavor to die to our self so that God can empower us to live and to love as he commands.

> What actually took place is this: I tried keeping rules and working my head off to please God, and it didn't work. So I quit being a "law man" so that I could be God's man. Christ's life showed me how, and enabled me to do it. I identified myself completely with him. Indeed, I have been crucified with Christ. My ego is no longer central. It is no longer important that I appear righteous before you or have your good opinion, and I am no longer driven to impress God. Christ lives in me. The life you see me living is not "mine," but it is lived by faith in the Son of God, who loved me and gave himself for me. I am not going to go back on that. Is it not clear to you that to go back to that old rule-keeping, peer-pleasing religion would be an abandonment of everything personal and free in my relationship with God? I refuse to do that, to repudiate God's grace. If a living relationship with God could come by rule-keeping, then Christ died unnecessarily. (Gal. 2:19–21 MSG)

This process begins with an honest examination of yourself. Especially the aspects of yourself that you generally prefer to ignore. I call them "my dirty little secrets." As we begin to get more real with ourselves, it is easy to begin to experience a great deal of disappointment and shame. We look at the real cause of our struggles and we discover that the world, the devil, and our flesh are the three main components.

This leads to the necessity of what we are calling a beautiful defeat. Two words that feel really uncomfortable together. Why defeat? And what could possibly be beautiful about this type of process? The first aspect of this defeat is the death of our flesh. This is not the death of our spirit (our essence), but rather those unhealthy desires that rage within us. We simply must put them to death, to become crucified with Christ, so that we can truly follow God the way he has called us to. This defeat is beautiful because of what happens when the flesh is diminished and his Spirit in us begins to guide us in our thoughts, our deeds, and our emotions.

Once this beautiful defeat occurs, we find ourselves not at the finish line but back at the starting line. And this time we must prepare for battle. Like a Navy SEAL we must learn to define, train for, and execute our mission. This leads us to the second beautiful defeat. This is the defeat of our enemies through love rather than any other tactic we have implemented in the past. When our flesh remains dead and God's Spirit operates through us, we are free to begin to become like him. The Bible says that God is love and this is how we must proceed. But we must learn to operate in love within a community. There are things we can look for in community as well as things we should offer to others.

I will finish with a final story.

The DeLong family lives in rural Ohio on a country road in an older home that is filled with love, faith, and family. The parents, Melia and Danton, have four children: son, Aramis, is seven years old, daughter Jubilee is five years old, daughter Hosannah is four years old, and youngest daughter Nalani is sixteen months old. Danton's thirty-year-old brother, Dijon, also lives with the family. Dijon, who is a quadriplegic, is filled with joy and wisdom that makes him a big part of this family.

It was Saturday night near bedtime, which meant family time. The family gathered in the main room downstairs for Bible stories and settling down before bed. Nalani, who is normally a ball of energy, seemed a bit more tired this night. Rather than struggling to stay still, she seemed content to rest in Melia's arms and she surprisingly fell asleep. Like many young children, she fought off her sleep and occasionally raised her head, saying, "Dada," and then she would fall back asleep.

Melia and Danton prayed with the children and then put Aramis, Jubilee, and Hosannah in bed for the night. Danton then fell asleep on the couch and Melia spent some extra cuddle time with her sleeping daughter, Nalani. She then placed Nalani on her husband's chest and cleaned up the kitchen, feeling that familiar nudge in her spirit to keep things in order. Around eleven o'clock that night, Melia put Nalani in her bed and went to bed herself.

The house was quiet the next morning. Melia and Danton

had decided to skip church this day as they were all exhausted from a busy week and from doing work on what would soon be their new house. Melia worked in the kitchen to get breakfast ready for the kids who would be waking up shortly. She then smiled to herself as she realized that Nalani had slept through the night for the first time. As Melia continued to make breakfast, she had an instinctual desire to check on her youngest. All the kids were still in bed, and Danton had begun to help Dijon get ready to start a new day. It was 9:00 a.m. when Melia peeked through the door to check on her sixteen-month-old baby girl.

She had looked in on her sleeping children hundreds of times, but for some reason she felt that something was just not right. She then took a closer look at Nalani, and she thought her eyes were playing tricks on her. It did not appear that Nalani was breathing. The young mother pulled back the blanket and put her ear to her daughter's mouth. Nothing. Until this point her mom had been simultaneously trying to check on her daughter and also not wake her up. Her strategy suddenly changed as she began to rub Nalani's chest and call out her name repeatedly.

Melia then screamed Danton's name as loudly as she could. Danton left Dijon and came to the room slightly before the other three children, who were awakened by her mommy's scream. Danton dialed 911 while Melia held Nalani's listless body on her shoulder.

Without shedding a tear, and in a calm tone that surprised her, Melia said to Aramis, Jubilee, and Hosannah, "I need you to go to the neighbor's house and I need you to obey me."

The children left as Danton took Nalani from Melia. As she handed her daughter to her husband, a distraught Melia said, "This is my fault." Her mind raced. Nalani was small, but she was healthy. *Did I feed her enough? Did she have an allergic reaction to something?*

"This is not your fault," Danton said firmly but lovingly as the reality began to set in that something was terribly wrong.

There were no signs of life in the tiny body. As hope faded that Nalani was alive, it returned with the notion that God could bring her back to life. But this would not be the case on this day. Nalani DeLong had gone on to heaven sometime during her sleep that night.

The ambulance arrived. Melia said to the paramedics at the house, "I do not know what you believe, but I believe in a God of miracles."

The coroner and the sheriff arrived soon after, and it became apparent that baby Nalani had passed away. They began to ask questions to try to determine what had happened. They would not find answers to their questions this day.

Melia and Danton were given a couple of hours with their daughter's body, and they spent the time crying, holding her, and begging God to intervene and bring their daughter back to life. Melia struggled with the question, how do you know when to let go? The thought she found most helpful was the image of her daughter being in God's arms and though it was hard on her as a mother, she knew Nalani was safe with her heavenly Father.

And then came the most difficult moment in Danton's life. He had to place Nalani's tiny body in the back of the hearse and shut the door. He knew that even though it was horrific to hold this lifeless body, he would never hold it again. He said that he could only trust, surrender, let go of his daughter's body, and know that God has a plan. He was crushed. The couple held each other and grieved deeply.

As they began to give the situation over to God in the hours that followed, he began to work on their hearts. Read the following Facebook post from Melia that was written on the day of Nalani's death:

Feel that you all should know where Danton and I (and kids) are at . . . we are heartbroken, shattered and broken in to innumerable pieces . . . beyond belief . . . yet . . . we still choose to praise the Lord in these darkest moments. The character of God does not change . . . only our circumstance or situation. Don't be offended if you can't reach us right now . . . we will keep you updated. We covet your prayers. Praising Jesus today.

And then her Facebook post to friends just two days later:

Still praising our LORD today! Come celebrate Nalani's new life with us on Friday at Vineyard Grace Fellowship on Route 13 south. Visiting beginning at 3 pm . . . service to begin at 7 pm. Food for out-of-towners and family/close friends. We are continually renewed by the Holy Spirit and are finding new strengths from His Word. Amazing peace. Feeling lifted up by the saints and overwhelmingly blessed by each of you. Danton and I are closer to our God and closer to each other. This kind of pain can tear relationships apart. We choose to be different. Our kids are stronger than we ever knew . . . Hosannah having a hard time understanding a bit, but we are speaking freely with them. Know this is only the beginning of these processes. Pray for wisdom for Danton and I on how to lead them through these times. HE HEALS THE BROKENHEARTED AND BINDS UP ALL THEIR WOUNDS! BLESSED BE THE NAME OF THE LORD TODAY AND EVERY DAY!

And then the next day (three days after the passing of her daughter):

Because some of you have asked . . . Nalani went to be with Jesus in her sleep. There is no reason . . . we have reports . . . "As you know, Mr. DeLong, your baby was perfect. We found nothing." We don't need reasons. We only need Jesus. His peace is perfect even in our suffering. If you don't know Him daily, deeply please come talk to us. We'd love to introduce you to a Father God that understands our struggles and yours. It's about relationship with him, that's truly the one and only reason we have any peace at all right now. Thanking the Lord for today and for ALL our blessings.

I met the DeLong family eleven days after the passing of Nalani DeLong on August 25, 2013, and was astounded by the intimacy they shared as a family that was completely based on an even deeper level of intimacy and surrender to the will of God. Melia shared that there are two kinds of whys that she had been thinking about with regard to Nalani. The first was based more on the physical cause of her daughter's death. At the time of this writing there is no known physical cause. But even if there were, Melia decided that she does not need to know this.

The second why is what we began to call the "why of God." What exactly was God's plan in all of this? Within days of this incident, Melia determined that she did not need to know this either. Melia, Danton, and Dijon would say repeatedly in a variety of different ways the same thing over and over:

God's character is unchanging and his ways are good.

Dijon said it this way: "Who am I to doubt the ways of the creator of the galaxy?"

Danton said, "I would like to understand, but I trust God and I know his ways are good."

Melia stated, "I do not need a why. I trust the Lord's sovereignty."

It is about surrendering. To surrender we must let go and have faith. We must let go of trying to get our way, the relentless pursuit of trying to meet our own needs and trying to understand everything that happens in our lives. And then there is having faith. We need to have faith in a God with a plan, in a God who knows the whys, and in a God who loves us more than we love ourselves and those close to us.

Listen closely to the words of this heartbroken and faith-filled couple as I sat with them at their kitchen table just days after the passing of their daughter "It is not about us. It is not about Nalani. And heaven is about more than us being with Nalani again. Heaven is about the worship of God, which is so much more important. We are people who do a lot of things wrong. We get short with our kids and with each other. We skip church sometimes. Sometimes we do not place our trust in God. But overall, we believe in a God that has our best interest in mind and we choose to have our lives based in his goodness."

When it comes to suffering and surrender, it all comes down to one thing. What will you place above your faith in God's character and his goodness? How deeply will you believe that God's character is unchanging and that his ways are good?

I, like the Delong family, am willing to stake my life on it.

TENTH STEP TO A SURRENDERED LIFE: Learn from those who have gone before you in your life and in the Bible.

Action Step

The book of Ecclesiastes says that there is nothing new under the sun, and 1 Corinthians 10:13 says that your struggles are common to man. Learn from the example of the DeLong family and other people that God has put in your life. Look for places in Scripture where surrender to God led to successful living. See if you can find a place in the Bible when surrender to God did not work. Hint: There is not one.

Prayer

God, please bring people into my life who can model for me the kind of surrender that you desire. Point out to me in Scripture the benefits of men and women who died to themselves and lived for you. Thank you for sending your Son, Jesus, who is the ultimate example of a surrendered life.

Acknowledgments

FIRST AND FOREMOST I WOULD LIKE TO THANK my heavenly Father. Not only did he save me spiritually at the cross and physically in a car accident, but he has provided just the right amount of difficulty and grace in my life to help me finally surrender to him.

Thank you to the body of Christ for your support, ideas, and love. Thank you also to Matt, Greg, Tracy, Shelly, and Bob for your help with the manuscript. Thank you, Thomas Nelson, for turning my ideas into a book.

To my family. This is what I was doing when I kept disappearing. Thank you for putting up with me. I love you.

Appendix 1

Ten Steps to a Surrendered Life

1. Know that the process of surrender is messy. (Introduction)

Action Step

Determine not to control your process of surrender. Commit to be open to whatever God and those close to you begin to show you. Do not try to align everything in the beginning of the process, but let things come together naturally for you further down the line.

Prayer

Father, help me not to chain myself to a vision of perfection. Teach me that I do not have to clean myself up to approach you. You know everything about me, so help me give all of it to you that you may make it clean. There is no reason for me to hold on to all that is tormenting me. Help me understand that struggle is a part of life that is not always an indicator of my disobedience. When I do act in ways that I should not, please forgive me. And when my hard times have nothing to do with my actions, please keep my mind and heart free to hear from you.

2. *Be honest about your existing struggles.* (Chapter 1)

Action Step

Make a list of the things in your life and about yourself that you really do not like. Write down what it is costing you to leave each issue unresolved. Begin to think about what it would be like to have peace in these areas even if the circumstances never change.

Prayer

Father, please help me more deeply understand that I do not need to perform for you. It is hard for me to believe that you designed me exactly the way you wanted me made. I worry more about what other people think they know about me than what you say is true about me. I want to let go of every burden, but I often find myself holding on tighter when I get scared.

Lord, where do you want me to start?

Show me one thing in my life that I can start with, and give me the courage to let go and turn it over to you. Help me learn to trust that being real with you and yielding my heart to you is always in my best interest. Thank you for loving and accepting me as I am.

3. *Know where your struggles come from.* (Chapters 2 and 3)

Action Step (devil, world)

Take some time to think about what you would do to keep you off track if you were the devil. What fears and thoughts would most derail you from the peace available to you in Christ? Be honest about what you truly live for. Identify at least three things that compete with God for the top spot in your life. Ask yourself, am I a lover of this world?

Prayer

God, please help me love you more than anything else in this world. Please also help me remember that the devil is real and he hates me as he hates you. The presence of your Spirit and the hope of heaven are far greater than anything I can find apart from you. Help me understand that I truly am a stranger in this land.

Action Step (the flesh)

Identify the emotions (e.g., anger, lust, fear) that tend to invade your spirit. What are the people, places, or things that tend to precede you being someone other than who you want to be? As you begin to identify these things, also begin to plan in advance how you will choose another course when they enter into your life in the future.

Prayer

God, please help me see my true enemies in my daily living. Make me aware of the devil and his lies, help me live for more than what this world has to offer, and help me be guided by your Spirit and not my flesh. I know that if I am living my life on autopilot none of this will occur. Help me set aside time each morning to talk to you and to hear from you both in prayer and in your Word. Please help me not only to be ready to battle but to be fighting the correct opponent in each moment of my life.

4. Determine to live through your struggles rather than around them. (Chapter 4)

Action Step

Try not to eliminate struggle, but ask God to help you discover his purpose in it.

Prayer

Lord, please forgive me for constantly running from you at the times when I need you most. Remind me of the times you have rescued me in the past. Thank you for showing me in the Bible where you did the same for your people. Help me realize that all life events are not about me and that there is much going on that I do not understand or even see. Most importantly, God, please help me remember that when you say all things will work together you are talking about your perfect plan for eternity and not my immediate need for comfort. Thank you for including me in your plans, and give me wisdom and insight so that I can play my role as you have designed it for me.

5. *Die daily.* (Chapter 5)

Action Step

Make a death certificate for yourself. Be creative and include whatever items make the most sense to you. Here are some items that are on mine: date of death, cause of death (my choice), do-not-resuscitate order, why I chose for my flesh to die, what I gained in my death.

Prayer

In this moment, God, I commit again to putting my flesh to death. I need more than self-control or more willpower. This is not about avoiding problems. I trust that as my Father, you know what is best for me and I place my trust in your ways rather than my own. Help me continually understand that you will not lead me in a way that is not best for me. Remind me of how well things went when I died on a given day and how wretched I feel about myself when I am driven by out-of-control desires. I know that I will have to do this again tomorrow, God, but let it be said of me today that I died to me and lived for you.

6. *Define your mission and wear your armor.* (Chapter 6)

Action Step

Take some time to think about what your day looks like if you view it as a battle, a series of events that will move you either further from or closer to God. Then think about each piece of armor that you just read about and how it would help you win these individual battles.

Prayer

Father, I have had many difficult days in my life. But the days where the difficulty could be traced to my decisions all had one thing in common: I did not put on my armor. Please help me to not only die each day to my desires but also to start each day preparing myself for the battle that is sure to come. You have given me everything I need to fight and you have even designed the battle to move me closer to you. But I ruin everything when I am not prepared as you would have me prepare. You have given me truth, righteousness, peace, faith, salvation, and your written Word. Help me respect and prepare for battle like a SEAL does for his mission. And let me consider success the fulfillment of your mission.

7. *Be part of a team.* (Chapter 7)

Action Step

Ask God to bring you safe people you can know and be known by, and when he does, make sure you take the initiative to connect with them. Also, find new ways to serve other people.

Prayer

God, I know you have designed me to be in community. Help me learn to not only be dependent on you but to depend on your people as well. Help me have deep, messy relationships as opposed to fake, sterile ones. Father, help me understand my need for you and my need for others. Please show me the people who need me and give me the courage to offer my help. Guide me into healthy community that is empowered by your spirit and your desires.

8. *Become addicted to your need for God.* (Chapter 8)

Action Step

Think about what things in your life you "must have." Is Jesus at the top of the list? You were designed to be dependent on him and to have him alive inside of you. Call upon his Spirit within you as you go through your day.

Prayer

Lord, please help me crave your presence. Put in me a desire to be with you and depend on you at all times. Draw me back when I begin to want other things more than you. Like the addict, make it difficult for me to function when I have not taken in enough of you. Thank you for your commitment to me that is in place regardless of my commitment to you. Thank you also for heaven where I will always be in your magnificent presence.

9. *Expect push back.* (Chapter 9)

Action Step

Increase your awareness that you are always in battle and so are your opponents. The devil never takes a day off, and you cannot either. Stay vigilant in your pursuit to be surrendered to God.

Prayer

God, please help me not to be complacent in my relationship with you. Give me the eyes to see my daily battle and help me be equipped with the tools that you provide for the fight. Bring people into my life to stand beside me. Thank you that you go before me and stand behind me. Help me not to be offended but to see my mistreatment as an opportunity to demonstrate grace. Fill me with your love so that I will treat others as you would. Thank you for being with me in the battle and also for providing the time and the place where we will no longer need to battle. The gift of heaven, eternity in your presence, is worth far more than any minor disturbance that comes my way for a finite moment. I want to battle for you every day, Father. Thank you for giving me everything I need for this fight.

10. Learn from those who have gone before you in your life and in the Bible. (Conclusion)

Action Step

The book of Ecclesiastes says that there is nothing new under the sun, and 1 Corinthians 10:13 says that your struggles are common to man. Learn from the example of the DeLong family and other people that God has put in your life. Look for places in Scripture where surrender to God led to successful living. See if you can find a place in the Bible when surrender to God did not work. Hint: There is not one.

Prayer

God, please bring people into my life who can model for me the kind of surrender that you desire. Point out to me in Scripture the benefits of men and women who died to themselves and lived for you. Thank you for sending your Son, Jesus, who is the ultimate example of a surrendered life.

Appendix 2

Ten Bible Verses on Surrender and Dying to Self

- For to me, to live is Christ and to die is gain. (Philippians 1:21)

- Therefore I urge you, brethren, by the mercies of God, to present your bodies a living and holy sacrifice, acceptable to God, which is your spiritual service of worship. (Romans 12:1 NASB)

- And He was saying to them all, "If anyone wishes to come after Me, he must deny himself, and take up his cross daily and follow Me." (Luke 9:23 NASB)

- "And he who does not take his cross and follow after Me is not worthy of Me." (Matthew 10:38 NASB)

- Now those who belong to Christ Jesus have crucified the flesh with its passions and desires. (Galatians 5:24 NASB)

- "For whoever wishes to save his life will lose it, but whoever loses his life for My sake and the gospel's will save it." (Mark 8:35 NASB)

- He Himself bore our sins in His body on the cross, so that we might die to sin and live to righteousness. (1 Peter 2:24 NASB)

- "I tell you the truth, unless a kernel of wheat is planted in the soil and dies, it remains alone. But its death will produce many new kernels—a plentiful harvest of new lives." (John 12:24 NLT)

- But may it never be that I would boast, except in the cross of our Lord Jesus Christ, through which the world has been crucified to me, and I to the world. (Galatians 6:14 NASB)

- For we who live are constantly being delivered over to death for Jesus' sake, so that the life of Jesus also may be manifested in our mortal flesh. (2 Corinthians 4:11 NASB)

About the Author

KEVIN MALARKEY IS A *NEW YORK TIMES* BEST-selling author and a sought-after national speaker.

Before his transition to writer and speaker, for many years Kevin owned a Christian psychotherapy practice, which included counseling with teens, adults, and families. Prior to his time in private practice, he worked in prisons, group homes, and residential treatment facilities.

Kevin has an undergraduate degree in sociology and religion and a graduate degree in clinical counseling. Kevin and his family live in Ohio.